W9-BMD-269

Realizing the
Promise of
21st-Century
Education

Realizing the Promise of
21ˢᵗ-Century Education

Education

An Owner's Manual

Bruce Joyce
Emily Calhoun

A JOINT PUBLICATION

CORWIN
A SAGE Company

FOR INFORMATION:

Corwin
A SAGE Company
2455 Teller Road
Thousand Oaks, California 91320
(800) 233-9936
Fax: (800) 417-2466
www.corwin.com

SAGE Ltd.
1 Oliver's Yard
55 City Road
London EC1Y 1SP
United Kingdom

SAGE India Pvt. Ltd.
B 1/I 1 Mohan Cooperative Industrial Area
Mathura Road, New Delhi 110 044
India

SAGE Asia-Pacific Pte. Ltd.
33 Pekin Street #02-01
Far East Square
Singapore 048763

Acquisitions Editor: Dan Alpert
Editorial Assistant: Sarah Bartlett
Production Editor: Libby Larson
Copy Editor: Paula L. Fleming
Typesetter: C&M Digitals (P) Ltd.
Proofreader: Theresa Kay
Cover Designer: Scott van Atta

Copyright © 2012 by Corwin

All rights reserved. When forms and sample documents are included, their use is authorized only by educators, local school sites, and/or noncommercial or nonprofit entities that have purchased the book. Except for that usage, no part of this book may be reproduced or utilized in any form or by any means, electronic or mechanical, including photocopying, recording, or by any information storage and retrieval system, without permission in writing from the publisher.

Printed in the United States of America.

Library of Congress Cataloging-in-Publication Data

Joyce, Bruce R.

Realizing the promise of 21st-century education : an owner's manual / Bruce Joyce, Emily Calhoun.

p. cm.
Includes bibliographical references and index.

ISBN 978-1-4129-8824-7 (pbk.)

1. Education—United States—History—21st century. I. Calhoun, Emily. II. Title.

LA209.2.J648 2012
370.973—dc23   2011022453

Certified Chain of Custody
SUSTAINABLE
FORESTRY   Promoting Sustainable Forestry
INITIATIVE   www.sfiprogram.org
             SFI-01268

SFI label applies to text stock

This book is printed on acid-free paper.

11 12 13 14 15 10 9 8 7 6 5 4 3 2 1

Preface

As Emily and I reached the last stages of working with the copyedited manuscript—essentially our last chance to improve it—we found ourselves sitting on our patio and asking each other whether we had made our messages clear. Back and forth the conversation went as we reflected on the last 18 months of study and writing and tried to put the primary theses and recommendations into a few words.

Where did our inquiry begin?

1. As educators, we were intrigued by the question of how schooling could capitalize on the remarkable development of digital information and communication technology (ICT) and ICT's massive influence in modern life across the world. ICT is defining the 21st century, not just in technological terms but through its pervasive influence on social relations and on how individuals, especially our youth, use their time. Rapid access to expansive knowledge bases provides information that affects the solving of problems large and small. In addition to making differences now, ICT promises future positive changes in many areas, including education.

2. However, we were struck by the uncertainty about how education would change itself: How would it respond to the opportunity to improve, not just by adopting elements of technology but by creating new ways of stimulating student learning? We were acutely aware that many school systems and school faculties struggle to identify priority areas for development and struggle to implement desirable changes they have identified.

   Some teachers and schools have just reached out and helped themselves and their children to expanded learning opportunities. They have changed their courses of study at the elementary and secondary levels, transformed homework into self-education, and connected the school and parents in new and productive ways. As a whole, however, educators have had difficulty deciding where to put energy; what devices to supply to classrooms, students, and homes; and how to go about incorporating ICT optimally in K–12 curriculum areas. Finding ways to proceed is very important; it is in fact of critical importance at this time.

3. We worry that, if schools and school districts do not move forcefully, teachers are likely to find themselves being monitors of distance courses that supplant campus instruction. Various agencies are currently building online and distance offerings as rapidly as they can. Secondary school students are increasingly completing off-campus courses and presenting them for graduation credit. Commercial developers are pressing the entire K–12 spectrum to adopt their offerings.

   Suddenly, teachers, schools, and districts are faced with an extraordinary choice.

   a. They can just let matters take their course and continue to conduct education as in the past.

   b. They can adopt distance offerings in the core areas and accept that developers will make decisions about content and process.

   c. Or they can use the opportunity to rebuild their K–12 programs, incorporating ICT to transform traditional campus offerings into hybrids that blend ICT into the core areas in service of stronger student learning.

4. This last option is our recommendation—the core of our position on policy and action. We believe that the best avenue for public education in Grades K through 12 is for faculties to organize themselves into development units that rework the campus offerings (current courses of study at the elementary and secondary levels) and build a new and better generation of education— essentially "hybrid" courses. In these courses, ICT resources are integrated into the implementation of quality curricula on current school campuses. Vast assets stand ready to be incorporated as educators at all levels, scholars, students, and professionals from around the world have access to each other at the click of a mouse or tap of a key. A new type of development-oriented professional development can easily be organized by building on the curriculum study and professional learning communities already in place in many school systems.

The promises of the 21st century can be realized through some hard but exhilarating work: exhilarating because redeveloping the educational program will propel teachers and administrators into high states of growth. *Their* learning will be broadened and accelerated to an extent that we have never seen.

5. We also realized that successful student learning will depend on making a major effort to improve literacy curriculum across Grades K–12 and across all subjects. Digital tools can help students develop good reading and writing skills by providing myriad opportunities for practice and application. Students with limited language arts and information literacy skills will struggle with ICT applications in the content areas. Learning platforms for these students must be strengthened.

   The literacy development of our students demands better professional development. Teachers presently are doing the best they can with what they know, but many of us will have to learn models of teaching that are currently unfamiliar if students' literacy is to improve rapidly enough to help them experience success in school and beyond.

6. Similarly, we came to understand that students will have to master cooperative/inductive/inquiry-oriented ways of learning—and *that* will not happen unless teachers master these ways of learning. (Everywhere we turned, we found another need for first-class professional development.) ICT skills can lead to information overload without increasing understanding of the concepts that form a domain of study. We need more instruction and curricula in which students gather information, learn to classify and organize it to increase understanding and use of concepts, and put their learning to work in solving problems and generating new ideas. Learning to work inductively and build inquiries supports both in-school and lifelong learning.

7. We agreed that our natural optimism was refreshed because we saw avenues for solving some problems that have been intractable. For example, low socioeconomic status (SES) has had a terrifying effect on the development of literacy for many and on their access to learning opportunities. Providing access to ICT, incorporating language arts and information literacy in all courses, and teaching students how to learn can ameliorate the SES-related problem seriously.

8. We wanted to address actions that school districts and school faculties can take now. We wanted not just to provide grand examples of what

is possible with extraordinary leadership and funding but to illustrate actions that any willing faculty can pursue. For the fulfillment of the opportunity to improve education will not come to us—we have to go to it. Whether the promise of the century will be realized in public K–12 education is primarily a matter of the will and work of those who reside there.

Bruce Joyce and Emily Calhoun
Saint Simons Island, Georgia

Contents

Just what are these new promises? Let's get clear about them and what we have to do to fulfill them. The authors' histories of studies of teaching and how teachers learn are combined with their studies of media technology and school renewal. The result is three basic ideas for incorporating contemporary technology to enrich curriculum, teaching, and student learning.

The new language of our times—"apps," virtual schools, virtual teaching, hybrids, infusion, and the like—will give us headaches unless we sort it out. We make a beginning here, with an emphasis on the implementation side of things. We emphasize New Libraries (which include print), new courses (hybrids, hybrids, and more hybrids), and accessible distance courses.

The development of information and communication technology is rapid and promises real changes as the school and home become platforms for learning and develop increasingly close partnerships in the process. Independent study will become more prominent. Also, we review here the 21st-century skills and add to and rework them into forms that we believe will be useful as information and communication technology is incorporated more fully into educational practice.

research in a never-ending quest for improvement and as a *fundamental and assumed* way of doing the work of education.

Here is the core of the process of implementation. The New Libraries already exist and are a key resource. Distance offerings are growing and growing in quality. *Now* teachers can build hybrid courses, ones based on the campus but drawing on the information and communication technology world. And, inductive/inquiry teaching will be the key to success in the new courses. Building hybrids will enable the promises to be fulfilled soon, and the skills to do so are within the repertoire of many teachers. Professional development will become *development,* and supporting school-based learning communities will become a major job of states and school districts.

The high school is ready for rejuvenation. The campus is ready for transformation, and hybrid courses and distance offerings will carry the cargo of new content and processes. Home and school will knit together in a partnership in which their interlocking platforms support high school students as never before.

Getting energy from professional associations in the school is a fine idea. Now the question is how to support the synergy of study groups and schoolwide action research. Here we urge a reciprocal professional development model.

We begin with an extensive scenario of Responsible Parties moving school and home into a high state of growth, then examine formative evaluation as an important development.

We envision a gradual—but not *too* gradual—evolution as the best of current practice is enhanced and new hybrid courses take their place in school and home.

Chapter Twelve: Direct, Performance-Based, Formative Assessment—Watching Learning Grow

Since the publication of the *Handbook of Formative and Summative Evaluation* (Bloom, Hastings, & Madaus, 1971), school improvement initiatives have virtually battled to increase the formative study of learning in classrooms and at the school, district, state, and national levels. Action research walks hand in hand with improvement. Test makers and the use of term-end and year-end grades on transcripts have drawn education toward summative evaluation. Federally mandated high-stakes testing has made summative evaluation pervasive and made formative study difficult. Equally important, test makers have rarely used performance measures, yet formative study requires them. We discuss the rationale and procedures for bringing about long-overdue change and the dilemmas faced.

Chapter Thirteen: An Optimistic Future

Provides a summary of the ideas that have coalesced to bring us to the optimistic position we hold and the belief that it is a fine time for educators to make *development* the most prominent aspect of professional development and add to curriculum and instruction the boosts that information and communication technology promises.

A coda reviews current popular literature, some of which contains worries that the coming of information and communication technology will be bad for our minds and our habits. We do not agree and say so. We see the advantages as far greater than the dangers.

Acknowledgments

We have again appreciated working with the Corwin organization in the production of this book. In particular, Dan Alpert, acquisitions editor, worked through the draft manuscript knowledgeably, thoughtfully, and assiduously. Paula Fleming edited the book and prepared it to be printed in an exemplary manner. Together, they make the best support we have ever had.

—BJ and EC

1

A New Chance to Live Our Dreams

A tantalizing wave of Information and Communication Technology (ICT) is flowing over us and beckoning us to actualize our most ambitious dreams for schooling—NOW.

> . . . Our Reflective Observer

A PROMISE WRIT LARGE

The major promise of our present time is to make an education that provides excellence for all. Both parts of the promise—*excellence* and *all*—are vital for our citizens, our society, and our place in the world.

As goals they build on the aspirations of our predecessors. Possibly none of them captured the promise better than Ortega y Gasset did in 1930 (1992). Paraphrasing slightly in translation . . .

> The mission of education is to enable people to live at the level of the highest ideas of their time.

By *live* he meant to have the inclination and ability to have a very high-quality life *and* contribute to the commonweal, both near at hand and far removed. He saw the academic and social as essential sides of the same coin.

The tremendous energy and powerful tools coming into our global society through the digital (read Information Communication Technology) revolution give fresh impetus to our age-old aspirations. Essentially, we can renew school renewal—and some of those new tools will give vitality to some high-potential curriculums and models of teaching that have had only limited dissemination in the past. Better curriculum and teaching will be the vehicle of change. Extensive professional development will be its engine.

Curriculum (what is taught) and instruction (how it is taught) can be elevated substantially. The social climate surrounding education will be enriched as more dimensions of communicating bring local students and parents closer together and connect them with cohorts all over the planet.

Although digital technology will add a wealth of information and ideas to the curriculum, its major impact will be on how students learn to think—how they build ideas and skills—and how they collaborate with one another.

As this is written, futurists and technology enthusiasts discuss possibilities and gnaw at the social implications. Mobile devices have enjoyed an extraordinary acceptance across the planet and are palpably changing human interaction and access to information.

However, education will *not* change much or improve greatly simply by making ICT more available in schools. We must rebuild curriculums and alter instruction if education is to improve. Educators, rather than technology providers, will need to do most of the "heavy lifting," although technical assistance is needed and distance courses can help greatly in some areas. Distance learning and virtual schools are changing the opportunities for learning in school and home. Although many current courses and programs were developed by commercial providers, we believe that the open source concept currently being advocated and currently promoted by the Gates and Packard foundations will result in more and better offerings.

The faculties in the schools that are leading the pack in the incorporation of ICT have done a great deal of hard and exhilarating work right where they live and teach. In those settings, home and school work together in fresh and more powerful ways. Interchanges like this are becoming common: *Parent post to Teacher's website.* I don't think Rory understands the arithmetic assignment. *Teacher to parent.* After reading your post, I reviewed the assignment with Rory. Does he understand it now?

The rigorous development in those schools needs to take place in *all* schools.

We will keep saying *all*. Most children from economically poor families have been terribly disadvantaged by the education available to them, and the spread of digital technology is very uneven. The disparities of the past will be magnified exponentially if educators do not turn that tide. Schools must ensure that access to good education, including the digital dimension, is equitable.

The infrastructure of schools, including technology on one hand and professional collaboration and study on the other, requires serious attention. With respect to technology, we are beginning to see schools that are wirelessly connected to homes, where all students are provided with laptops and smartphones upon registration and where interactive whiteboards and their successor devices are in all instructional settings. These devices run on software that makes self-instruction a central dimension of schooling. At the same time, decades of experience with successful and unsuccessful school improvement initiatives have made it clear that high-quality professional development should be considered part of the essential infrastructure—the motor that drives the improvement of curriculum and teaching.

The territory of this book is the needed work to fulfill the tremendous promise of this time. We intend it to outline avenues to development that can be done right now as schools, districts, states, and federal agencies redevelop curriculum and teaching. The incorporation of digital technology can serve as a springboard toward a renewal of school renewal.

We write from our view of the processes needed to begin to capitalize on ICT. A good many resources will be mentioned, and an annotated bibliography is provided to guide the reader to the help available. But avenues for development make up the core of this work.

WHAT WE HAVE LEARNED ABOUT TEACHERS, TECHNOLOGY, AND PROFESSIONAL DEVELOPMENT

The incorporation of media into schooling has been a century-old process. And we, the authors, have been involved in this process for a good many years. We have been paying attention to teachers and ways of teaching for a very long time. Collecting data on how people teach—and how they *might* teach—became the focus of our work, individually and together.

Early on, we began to study the ways teachers teach and alternative ways of teaching. In our early careers, the study of teaching and learning had attracted a considerable number of researchers. They were producing a great deal of information about how teaching is usually practiced and about alternative approaches to teaching. Most of the researchers were looking for a few solid principles that would define good teaching in general—teaching for all purposes.

However, students need to pursue many objectives. Innovative teacher-scholars had generated a variety of approaches to teaching that achieved different objectives or, sometimes, accomplished similar objectives but in different ways. As Bruce and his colleagues studied those approaches, it became clear that rather than there existing a few overriding principles of all-purpose teaching, there were a number of valid models, grounded in beliefs and supported by research. We studied them, clarified the teacher and student skills needed to use them, and conducted research on them, particularly on their interaction with the diverse learning styles of students. The idea that there is a storehouse of models is an enduring theme of our work to the present (see Joyce, Weil, & Calhoun, 2009). Our inquiries on how learning styles interact with alternative models of teaching were particularly influenced by the conceptual-level model developed by Harvey, Hunt, and Schroder (1961). We became close colleagues with David Hunt while conducting a long series of studies of student response to alternative learning environments (see Hunt & Sullivan, 1974). Emily built on the work of many earlier educators such as Gagne, Taba, and Stauffer in developing a multimodel approach to teaching beginning reading and writing (Calhoun, 1999). An important principle undergirding this work is that, to learn and use complex skills, students need to see them, understand them, and practice them so that these skills become a natural part of the learning repertoire.

Another Focus: How Teachers Learn

Another theme in our careers has been the study of how teachers learn. In the 1970s, many educators believed individual teachers' methods were a product of their personalities. The concept of professional repertoire was new, and many doubted that new teachers could learn approaches to teaching that did not fit with their personalities. However, there was a dearth of data about how teachers learn.

We became part of a community that focused on the nature of competence in teaching. That community conducted extensive research to learn whether teachers could learn to teach in ways different from the ones they "naturally" brought to teaching. We found that teacher candidates could acquire a wide professional repertoire, one far beyond the recitation model that has historically dominated teaching. Personality was a factor, but not a limiting one (see Harvey et al., 1961; Joyce, Peck, & Brown, 1981).

How Do Experienced Teachers Learn?
Implications for Professional Development

We extended the study of preservice education to professional development contexts. It turned out that experienced teachers also could extend their repertoires considerably. Furthermore, they could increase the achievement of their students significantly by using models more appropriate to the course goals, whether those of the teachers or the students, and by being better able to accommodate teaching styles and learning styles (see Joyce & Showers, 2002).

However, teachers do not expand their repertoires simply by reading about them or listening to talks about them. We learned that teachers acquired new teaching strategies by studying the rationales of those strategies, watching and analyzing several (a dozen or more is best) demonstrations, and preparing practice in the core curriculum areas. And transferring new practices into their active repertoires took time and collegial companionship. To facilitate transfer, we developed peer coaching—teachers helping each other use their new learning. Implementation rates rose from about 10 percent after traditional professional development workshops to about 90 percent when peer coaching was employed after the theory-demonstration-practice strategy was used in workshops.

Importantly, this line of work demonstrated that teachers have the capacity to add considerably to their repertoire—that they are not trapped in a narrow range of teaching strategies (see Joyce & Showers, 2002). This finding is particularly relevant to the current challenge to incorporate new media into the curriculum. As with students, for teachers to learn complex new skills, they need to see them, understand them, and practice them until the skills become a comfortable part of their teaching/learning repertoire. Essentially, teachers need to become comfortable in a digital environment.

School Improvement of Size: Concentrating on Literacy

In the last few years, we have been drawn toward collaborative school improvement projects with schools and school districts where knowledge of professional development, models of teaching, and action research are brought together. These projects have demonstrated the considerable magnitude of increase in student learning that is possible within relatively short periods when students are taught better tools for learning (see Joyce & Calhoun, 1996). Emily's extensive studies of action research in more than 100 schools were important in helping us estimate the amount of support necessary for teacher and administrator leaders as inquiry modes are used in school renewal.

We have concentrated on literacy in Grades K–3 and in a Grades 3–12 curriculum for struggling readers. With our colleagues in Canada, we have generated evidence that the use of the Picture Word Inductive Model of Teaching (Calhoun, 1999) as the core of the literacy curriculum can generate considerable rises in rates of learning to read and write (see Joyce & Calhoun, 2010, for reports of the studies). In the Northern Lights School Division in Alberta, we and Marilyn and Walter Hrycauk have followed for eight years kindergarten students who were taught to read. During that time the students have, year by year, increased their lead over comparison groups of students. To help others conduct action research on the teaching of reading, Emily has authored a book focusing on the assessment of reading curriculum and instruction in schools and class-rooms (Calhoun, 2004). We continue to marvel at the learning capacity of both novice and experienced teachers.

TECHNOLOGY AND EDUCATIONAL PRACTICE

Media has been a recurrent component of this work, reminding us that both electronic media and digital technology have been available and used in some settings for a long time. Bruce was connected with innovators in educational media, including *Sesame Street*, and wrote extensively about the integration of media in schooling (see Joyce, 1967, 1972). To support curriculum research, he and his colleagues developed data banks for children's study of cultures and studied students' inquiry into cultures foreign to them. The work anticipated the development of digitized data banks as the technology became available. In the 1970s, Bruce directed teacher education programs in which teams of teacher candidates and cooperating teachers videotaped lessons as they learned to use research-based models of teaching. In seminars, they studied their lessons and used observational systems for studying teaching that resulted in data being placed in computer files. Students and faculties used those files to track the developing teaching styles and, as student learning was studied, to inquire into whether various patterns of teaching and models were related to effects on student achievement. These data were important in our learning that teacher candidates and their cooperating teachers could master a considerable range of models of teaching and use them effectively.

Very few teacher education programs used electronic media to the extent we and our colleagues did at that time (see Joyce & Clift, 1984)—and only a handful do today but for us and our colleagues, the study of various models of teaching has continued. From that research we identify those ways of teaching that are most promising for integrating electronic technologies into the curriculum.

The learning from our professional work brings us to where we are now.

Throughout the book, the reader will find that the lessons from these histories guide our approach to an integration of technology that can generate great improvement in what students learn and how they learn. The incorporation of digital technology into schooling can be accomplished by paying attention to just three straightforward propositions.

1. Incorporating digital technologies into the learning environment begins as teachers rework courses (K–12) to take advantage of the "New Libraries" (a term we devised to describe the vast collection of resources

available on the Internet) and distance learning offerings. *The needed teachers' skills are not exotic or difficult to learn.* Many have been familiar for years, if underimplemented. The skills needed in the near term to incorporate electronic digital technologies into educational practice are fundamental ones on which others can be built. The futurists talk about skills at the level of rocket science, but the basic work of redeveloping courses, creating hybrids, and building online distance offerings, including online courses, is fundamentally within the range of most folks who can browse the web competently. Courses need to help students see, understand, and practice the highest level of learning/living skills.

2. Teachers have plenty of capacity to learn what is needed and to do so in the process of rebuilding courses and finding innovative ways of helping home and school work together. As their skills grow, so will their ability to learn more. They will nurture the "digital natives" (Prensky, 2010) who come to them, and they will welcome all their other students into the digital world.

3. Professional development will be the key to the extent to which redevelopment of the learning environment takes place. School improvement has never more depended on it. The care and feeding of school faculties has to be rejuvenated and made much stronger. Schools will initiate some changes, and districts will initiate other changes from their perspective.

Teachers learn new ways of teaching by seeing them, understanding them, and practicing them. Professional development that includes these elements is very, very successful because of the learning capacity of teachers.

2 Terms of Convenience

Building a New Language for Teaching and Learning

Some familiar terms, like library *and* librarian, *will have new meaning. Print and Internet resources will mingle and each will serve the other. A frightening study indicated that schools were cutting library staffs as part of their budgetary problems (Blankinship, 2010). Actually, we will need librarians more than ever to help students and teachers access combinations of print and digital resources.*

. . . Our Reflective Observer

Three key terms, hybrid course, blending, *and* infusion, *drive the school improvement efforts as we build Information Communication Technology (ICT) into our schools. We are not ready to float through cyberspace into virtual schools inhabited entirely by virtual teaching, although some exist in both public and commercial forms. But we are ready for some down-to-earth improvement of our courses, turning campus courses into hybrids by connecting them to the New Libraries, blending digital and campus instruction and infusing digital technology into the school and home learning platforms.*

. . . Our Technology Friend

We are wading into a moving river of educational and social change. The water is more than a little murky, but it is loaded with nutrients.

Just sorting out terms takes some effort. Sometimes the rhetoric about Information Communication Technology (ICT) makes it seem like nothing will be recognizable in the aftermath of a cyberrevolution. Not so. Many of our new devices (both machines and methods) are built on ones that have existed for quite a long time. The written letter carried by messenger and then the postal service, the book, the newspaper, the words of courtship, have been added to and transformed in marvelous ways. Some old things will be put on the shelves of antiquity. Some will put on new clothes. Thus far, the familiar skills of literacy have been made more and more important as ICT advances.

> *Authors' note:* Throughout the book, we will keep reminding ourselves that literacy is a vital part of the promise. Sometimes we hear it said that the literacy skills in the cyberworld will be different from the skills used to access the print media. Not so. But high-level literacy skills will be needed, and they must be integrated with the digital tools for retrieving and organizing information. As hybrids are developed, the content of the curriculum in reading will be more powerful and complex than before. Students and teachers will access both print and Internet libraries comfortably.

As we write, many districts, schools, and teachers are incorporating various aspects of ICT into their work. Sometimes they add a new piece of equipment, like an interactive whiteboard. Sometimes they provide additional professional development support. A small percentage of schools have really and truly infused technology *throughout* the learning process.

And more than a few teachers are making elaborate changes in their work. As they talk about what they are doing, new terms fly through the air. We don't think that strict standardization is necessary, but we need to clarify the terms we use regularly, particularly those we invented or adopted.

To talk to each other, we use some old terms, have adopted some new ones, and have invented a few to denote some new concepts, doing so for our convenience and hopefully for our readers. Our major categories are these:

- Components of education
- New educational resources
- Terms referring to teaching and assessment
- The professional learning platform

ON COMPONENTS OF EDUCATION

Course. This term has long been used in secondary and higher education. We use it also in primary and middle education, referring to planned activities in academic curriculum areas, and find the term very useful.

Within the curriculum areas in the primary grades we can think of a unit or *course* on neighborhood. In high school, for example, we can think of the *course* on physics. Students can take courses on campus, at home, or combinations thereof. Workshops and other short offerings can also be taken in many forms and venues, including on-line. Physical education, the visual and fine arts, media, and technology can all be wonderfully enhanced with ICT applications. In many schools, the practical arts and industrial technology have led the way in innovation.

Core curriculum area refers to the major traditional curriculum groups: English language arts, particularly reading and writing and literature; social studies; mathematics and arithmetic; science, including the specific sciences; and second or third languages.

Campus-based courses refer to offerings on a physical campus of some sort. ICT devices or resources such as interactive whiteboards may be included in campus-based courses.

In *hybrid courses*, face-to-face, campus-based sessions are deliberately integrated with World Wide Web libraries and other distance resources. Sometimes the term *blended* is used to refer to hybrid courses, but we prefer *hybrid* as we think of the variety of ways the New Libraries, campus sessions, and resource-based offerings can be combined. To make ICT pay off, campus courses need to be rebuilt, not just given access to the web. As you will see, we find the term *hybrid* to be very useful when thinking about curriculum design and development. It may be that the proper usage will be that "we blend in order to make hybrids." In any event, we repeat: the core courses, including the primary curriculum areas, need to be reconstructed, and ICT gives us a great opportunity to do that.

Resource-based education refers to opportunities for the learner to use data sources, media-based materials (including but not solely online courses) for self-guided or assisted inquiry. Importantly, a significant part of a course can consist of inquiry by the students—garden-variety term paper assignments are an age-old example, but the availability of ICT resources makes the very term feel old-fashioned. Thesis writing has generally been resource based. Although the term *online course* is popular, we find *resource-based* to be far more useful when discussing the process of rebuilding existing courses.

Distance education is the variety of resource-based offerings that are largely ICT based. Online and televised courses are the most common, but this area is like a garden of wild flowers. All sorts of varieties are appearing.

Twenty-first-century skills refers to the half dozen competencies that have been much publicized as essentials for the emerging century. We believe that they are best taught in the context of hybrid courses. Chapter Six deals with these in some depth, but they bear mentioning here:

- ICT literacy
- Cultural literacy and global awareness
- Collaborative and cooperative skills
- Personal and social responsibility
- Creativity and innovation
- Critical thinking and problem solving

Very present in the current literature on school renewal, these can be used effectively as courses and curricula are redeveloped. They represent objectives for students, and they fit well with the objective of an excellent education for all. The job of educators is to figure out what kinds of teaching/learning models will accomplish these objectives and then how to implement those methods of instruction.

THE CONCEPT OF CONNECTED TEACHING

The U.S. Department of Education's educational technology plan was released in March 2010, and the title itself tells us that it is on the side of the fervent optimists: *Transforming American Education: Learning Powered by Technology.*

The document is zealously devoted to providing students and teachers with access to the best of ICT and developing better and better distance courses. This vision is clearest with respect to changing the situation of teachers, moving from isolation to what is termed "Connected Teaching." Essentially, the Department of Education projects a situation in which teachers are connected to one another and can share ideas, talk (blog, Skype) together, and be fed through professional development distance sources.

That the federal government is not just on board with expanding the ICT world but is planning to make major initiatives in education is very encouraging. Until there is an economic recovery of considerable magnitude, states and local agencies are unlikely to make the investments that are needed now. In fact, when we encounter districts that are actually considering closing school libraries, we are nearly terrified. On the other hand, Bruce visited a school district recently where all classrooms are provided with interactive whiteboards.

Much needs to be done to flesh out the Department of Education's vision, but we are pleased with the goals and seriousness of the plan.

> We have worked with the U.S. Department of Defense Education Activity (DoDEA) for more than 20 years. During those years, its staffs worked hard to deliver excellent education in the ninth largest school system in the country. A unique characteristic, of course, is that its schools are scattered throughout the world, serving the dependents of servicemen and servicewomen and, to a lesser extent, the populations near the overseas military bases. The DoDEA curriculum guides were more clearly standardized than much of what we've seen in our era when "benchmarks and standards" have become a mantra.
>
> Part of the strength of the curriculum guides was in response to the anxiety of parents that their children, moved from place to place on the military bases, would encounter different curricula at each new post. But they also addressed parents' concern that should they leave the military or be in a posting where DoDEA schools were not available, their children would be disadvantaged as they attended public schools.
>
> One of the persistent problems was that transitions are often in stages. The family moves from Fort Smith, Arkansas, to Fort Sam Houston–San Antonio, Texas, for two months of training for the soldier, then to Wiesbaden in Germany for a three-year stint. There was no way that the schools could be synchronized down to the exact pages in the textbook, but the curricula could match fairly well; the schools were also accustomed to the continual entrance of new students.
>
> Now, DoDEA is introducing (February 2011) a virtual school, which will help fill the gaps. A wide range of high school courses is included. Students may take those that are not offered in a school they attend except when in transition (as in the above example). The student in the scenario above can leave Fort Smith, keep up with his or her courses on the way to and while in San Antonio, study on the way to Germany, and settle down before a computer in Wiesbaden.
>
> Well, why not?

THE COMMON CORE STANDARDS

For several decades, there has been a strong movement to generate state and national curriculum standards and the mechanisms to ensure their implementation. The Council of Chief State School Officers and the National Governors Association have paid particular attention to content standards. They examined the standards of the 50 states and the District of Columbia and rated them for their rigor and probability of having a positive effect on student learning. In June of 2010, the Common Core State Standards for English Language Arts and Mathematics were released. As we go to press, nearly all the states and the District of Columbia have adopted the Common Core State Standards in place of their existing (state) standards (see www.corestandards.org). Some advocates of new standards and benchmarks believe that these standards should mirror the standards of the highest-achieving countries, educationally speaking. Actually, the curricula of the highest-achieving are very similar to ours. What the new standards do reflect is the framework of the 21st-century skills. They strongly support conceptual teaching and the development of creativity. Many are vague about how ICT might be incorporated, although they mention it.

A key question is whether the adopters of the Common Core standards will also invest in the professional development needed to upgrade education. To do so, they need to reconcile the philosophies of the currently fashionable bottom-up models of professional development, such as those centered on professional learning communities and coaching, with the needs of stronger standards or ones emphasizing new skills. The professional learning community and coaching models emphasize the current repertoire of teachers' skills. New standards and digital needs may require a new repertoire. As online courses and virtual schools are developed, nearly all of them will use the standards and benchmarks as the outlines for their courses, assessments, and materials. And, the standards can be virtual outlines for virtual schools.

NEW, EXPANDED RESOURCES

We shaped a number of terms in which we use the word *new*.

New Library refers to the big information base to which we are connected. The New Library includes the old (brick-and-mortar) libraries and improved access to their collections. As they are linked, we come closer to having a universal library that includes their digital collections. Importantly, many libraries have digitized huge collections of pictures, film and video material, and visual arts (see Blecksmith, 2008, for a fine summary). Children who are just learning to read can access those collections. Special mention needs be given to the Library of Congress. The size of its digitized collections is truly remarkable.

Platforms for learning refers to the concept of schools and homes as opportunity centers—places where we actively seek out opportunities for education, rather than waiting for it to be delivered. Homes that are equipped with computers and other digital devices and are wired for access to the

Internet become enhanced learning centers. Home and school will become platforms for learning.

New Courses refers to resource-based courses designed for self-education, as well as hybrid courses.

Both the New Library and the New Courses are included in *open education resources (OER)*, where courses are online and free except for materials (see www.oercommons.org). The William and Flora Hewlett Foundation has invested substantially in the development of OER materials and access to them. Due to the investment by the foundation, syllabi and other materials from nearly 1,600 courses are available. Only 33 include videos, however, even of lectures. OER materials are resources, and only some are complete courses. Nonetheless, OER has a bright future and builds on developments in existence before the foundations got involved. Quality sites for teachers continue to be added to our storehouse, such as the National Science Digital Library (www.nsdl.org) designed to support teachers K–12.

TERMS REFERRING TO TEACHING AND ASSESSMENT

Models of teaching refers to theory- and research-based, tested approaches to teaching.

In the current literature, we see the term *project-based* to mean that students try to solve a problem or build a product. The students can collaborate from a variety of settings or be together on one campus.

In *performance-based assessment*, behavior is measured directly. This contrasts with tests whose scores are inferences about performance. For example, a performance-based assessment of reading asks the student to read real books; contrast this to a test made up of items, such as multiple-choice or true-false items, that deal with aspects of reading but do not require real-life performance.

Instructor is used interchangeably with *teacher* and *facilitator*.

A *digital textbook* or *ebook* can be a print textbook available in digital files or a document that is enriched to include hyperlinks, video clips, and other varieties of media. Many current textbooks will soon become online courses. However, we should not expect ebooks to replace print books entirely (see the interesting article on students' preference for print textbooks on some campuses; Foderaro, 2010). However, ebooks can contain material that will not be accommodated in a print book, and they should be more than just a digitized print book. And, open source tools such as Moodle (www.moodle .org) make it easy for teachers to work together in developing curriculum materials for use by students within and beyond their classrooms.

THE PROFESSIONAL LEARNING PLATFORM

We think we need a new term to fit the changing concepts of professional development, but we don't have a good one yet. Learning Forward (formerly National Staff Development Council) uses the term the *learning school* to capture its vision of a place where teachers and students engage in continual learning. In Chapter Ten, we introduce two terms, *professional learning platform* and *reciprocal professional development. Reciprocal professional development* expresses a new way of looking at internal and external resources. For example, in the school, a team develops a New Course for its students. The team decides to access help from a university or R & D center. The two agencies work reciprocally as the team helps the center formulate its products or services and the center gives team members access to externally developed resources. Or a school team contacts a state resource center for help implementing a summer reading program. Or a state asks a district to conduct a pilot study of professional development relative to a new curriculum.

We favor combinations of models of professional development but certainly *action research* at all levels. In upcoming years, professional development needs to focus on the structure of the curriculum and the development of hybrid courses where print and cyber literacy are embedded.

Infusion refers to making the new technologies an integral part of the curricular and instructional process. Schools that take the bull by the horns use the term to indicate that they expect the technology to pervade the learning environment.

Speaking of which, this is a good place to stop defining and get to the business at hand.

WHAT TO DO NOW

From this beginning, we examine what schools and school districts need to do now to reinvent themselves by capitalizing on the opportunities presented by the development of relevant technologies. Now, let's discuss our considerable opportunities.

Part I

A Considerable Opportunity

When I emailed my students' parents with the question "What countries would you like to explore—even to visit?" I had no idea what a variety would be suggested. I then gave the list to my fifth-grade students without telling them that it was a compilation of ideas from their parents. I asked them to search for information, making sure that certain types (size, population, gross national product) were included, and then to write a description of what one might find by traveling there. We made a kind of multimedia travel book and presented it to the parents.

There are going to be a lot of families discussing whether they can organize the time and resources for some real as well as virtual travel. Whatever they do, the parents asked for more, and my young digital inquirers are making slide shows and videos as this project takes on a life of its own.

. . . Our Collegial Teacher

Current media and communications technology stands on the shoulders of a large base of predecessors. Sesame Street has celebrated its 50th birthday, and distance-education-based The Open University is now 45 and has graduated upwards of 3,000,000 students in the UK.

We know more than we may realize about how to implement technology and, while new learning is certainly needed, the best is yet to come.

. . . Our Reflective Observer

In order to achieve the overarching goal of a high-quality education for all students, educators must commit to some very serious development work at the school and district levels, with support from those at the state and federal levels. Incorporating digital technology provides a great opportunity for *renewing school renewal.* It also can potentially help us solve some old and vexing problems. We should improve learning capacity by teaching students to work in a cooperative/inductive/inquiry mode. Literacy will improve. If we do it right, SES differences will be diminished or eliminated. We will be making school and home into partnered platforms that support excellence. We will fill them with newly designed courses, which we call "hybrids" because they build on the best of on-campus offerings and blend in the wonderful New Libraries. We will select from the distance offerings, those that are available now and the exponentially greater numbers of the future.

Education reform may strike some as daunting because of the scale of our national educational enterprise. Consider the following:

- Education is 7.6 percent of per capita gross domestic product.
- Our schools serve 55 million kids . . .
- . . . through 4 million teachers and paraprofessionals . . .
  ○ (That's one adult for every 12 students.)
- . . . and 150,000 school administrators.
- Of enrollees in Grade 9, about two-thirds graduate in four years.
- At the undergraduate level, we have 7,000,000 men in college presently and more than 10,000,000 women; the average male takes seven years to graduate, while the average female takes about five years.
- Special education enrolls about one in seven students. Few exit.
- For the nation as a whole, about 70 percent of our students are able to read independently by Grade 4. In some schools, all can. In the average suburb, about 80 percent can. In *some* city schools, only 30 percent can.

Yet, we have low-socioeconomic status (SES) schools whose students learn to read better than those in the average suburban schools (see Harkreader & Weathersby, 1998; Iowa Association of School Boards, 2007). We have some fine schools—and the capacity to make them *all* that good.

Those who claim that our best schools do not produce world-class students are simply dead wrong. As are those who believe that we can solve our problems by simply emulating the practices of other countries. However, we concur that there is significant room for improvement.

3 Educating at the Level of the Highest Ideas of Our Time

Enlarging Moral Purpose in the Pursuit of Equity and Excellence

Civilization did not begin the day we were born. Ideas thought out and fought for long ago are the wind beneath our wings.

As we lean our backs and minds into the job of building the finest possible education, we can look behind us in time and find a powerful community of spokespersons for an education vigorous both socially and intellectually. Plato, Aristotle, Aurelius, Aquinas will come to everyone's mind. And Comenius, Rousseau, Locke, the Encyclopedists, Jefferson, Mann, Barnard, Du Bois, Whitehead, Dewey. . . . As women have had more voice, think of Abigail Adams, Margaret Sanger, Maria Montessori, Eleanor Roosevelt, Simone de Beauvoir . . . and others too numerous to mention. They are changing the world.

Our predecessors were creating, in their own times, a real base for 21st-century thinking about education and passed it along for us to build upon. The heritage is with us, refreshed by each generation as it adds new ideas and tools.

Amazingly, until recently, thinkers built their ideas when just a tiny fraction of the population had access to any formal education and powerful forces wanted to make sure education would always be denied to most people. Even today in our nation, fulfilling their ideas requires changes, such as helping students generate new ways of thinking, that face serious opposition from proponents of a conforming education.

The great achievement of American education was the establishment of the common school and locating it in all the communities of the nation. Yet, we did not rush to ensure equality in higher education.

The GI Bill at the end of World War II made higher education a reachable birthright and transformed the social system, answering George Counts's (1932/1978) great question, "Dare the schools build a new social order?" Social participation and upward mobility through education were taken to a remarkable new level. Simultaneously, an underclass was spawned in the towns and cities to create appalling levels of inequality between the new middle class and those who were left behind. The local schools that have accomplished so much have not been able to overcome this terrible gap.

At the core of the purpose of education, fulfilling the promise of those highest ideas, is a focus on capacity: the cognitive, social, and moral intelligences.

We will now find the moral fiber to succeed. Make no mistake, while the coming of ICT is very important, learning to elevate schooling and sheer grit will determine the end game.

Building education around the enhancement of intelligence—inquiry-oriented, inductive, problem-solving processes—will be triggered by the new environments, the media-rich environments, that are the product of the intelligent behavior on which we will build.

AN IMPORTANT MESSAGE FROM THE MAKER: HUMANS HAVE TREMENDOUS ADAPTIVE CAPACITY

Emily often quotes the incisive Chinese proverb: Act your way into believing and then believe your way into action. The best ideas may *require* action if we truly believe them. Let's apply this wisdom to present and emerging views about the capability of teachers as learners and about human capability to change and adapt in general.

Teachers as Learners

In our book *Models of Professional Development*, we stressed again and again that teachers (educators) have wonderful learning capacity (Joyce &

Calhoun, 2010). In study after study, teachers have learned models of teaching and curriculum that expanded their repertoires (see the summaries in Joyce et al., 2009). Another finding from the large literature on teachers as learners is that the context of the workplace has a great effect on whether a new repertoire will be used in such as way that it enhances student learning. In other words, school and district officials have to focus on providing those conditions. We will revisit this topic again, because not every type of professional development generates new repertoire and not every well-intended attempt to facilitate implementation accomplishes its aim.

For now, we feel compelled to remind policy makers, state and federal organizers, district and school leaders, and, most of all, teachers that they can learn new things quite capably. *The educational promises of the 21st century depend on professionals learning new things so that students can learn new things.* Some powerful voices would create a technologized educational system where creativity by teachers and students would not be prized. An elaborate core curriculum would be developed, the materials developed to implement it, and the tests created to assess it, A Brave New World, indeed, with the curriculum makers in charge. They ignore the simple truth that education is a collective human enterprise. Our new tools should enhance rather than diminish what people need to do together and how they need to help each other.

Much of the current literature on school improvement appears to have been written by folks who have not absorbed these fundamental truths. Articles and books by a variety of pundits are filled with comments about things schools are not doing now and skepticism about teachers' capability and motivation. We are beginning to wonder whether an aura of pessimism has been created by some of the very folks who champion school improvement.

In other words, if you find yourself becoming pessimistic about how well teachers can handle the demands of the times, be mindful that the considerable amount of grim prose can lead to a self-fulfilling prophecy. Getting back to the proverb, the consequence has been that you can think yourself into *inaction.*

Let's exorcise that ghost.

People as Cultural Learners and Adaptors

Diversity is a great thing rather than a problem. Differences are the spice in our diet. Fortunately, wonderful messages about the adaptive, quality-seeking nature of our species are proliferating.

Globalization has brought migration with it. Many people have migrated to nations with different cultural patterns and languages than the ones they grew up with. And their ability to learn new cultures and languages and become successful in other places is a masterpiece of human capacity.

Over the years, we have been inspired by the example of the Vietnamese diaspora. Following a devastating, divisive war, one-fortieth of the population migrated. Today, more than 7 million live in other countries: 1.6 million are in the United States; 1.5 million are in Australia and about that many in Canada; more than 250,000 are in France; 150,000 in Russia; 80,000 in Germany; 40,000–60,000 in the Czech Republic, Japan, and the UK; and 10,000 or so in each of the Scandinavian countries.

As a population, these émigrés landed in places with cultures and languages that were radically different from their own. Yet many of the children became high achievers in their new schools! What a testimony to the inborn drive to build quality lives—*and to do so by learning!* Many migrating populations have provided similar testimony. We strongly believe that the key to teaching diverse populations is to capitalize on the energy and rich variety they bring to our schools. Let's celebrate human capacity and drive!

We have come to the above beliefs about the nature of the skills needed to be implemented in the near term, the capacity of educators, and how educators can seize the moment to take advantage of available technologies by building hybrid courses and shaping school and home as platforms for learning.

WE CAN DO IT NOW!

The New School actually exists, both in prototype form and in reality. The job for most of us is to build the reality in our own settings. As we stated previously, the skills needed to integrate digital technology are not exotic or difficult to master. Some authors suggest that the skills needed to access ICT are obscure, even weird. They even intimate that one must grow up with digital skills to thoroughly master them, in the manner of acquiring a language. In reality, educators have been absorbing these competencies for quite a while and are already primed to infuse digital technology across their practices. And the new skills can build on developments that have been accumulating for several decades. Counterintuitive as it may seem, the core of the new curriculum is good old teaching and learning. For years, we studied the models of teaching as a repertoire for teachers and goals for students. We know how to create the conditions that make it easy for teachers to ease into using them and learn how to use them to create platforms for learning and hybrid courses. The technological applications needed by educators right now and for the immediate future are not hard to learn, and they build on ones that nearly every teacher has already mastered.

4 Promises

Educational Renewal Is Getting a Lift

We have known for a very long time that inductive, inquiry-centered curriculums and models of teaching actually improve intelligences, the social and moral as well as the cognitive. Add the advantages of the digital tools, and promises abound. The catch is that learning to capitalize on the ICT tools requires learning to teach inductively.

. . . Our Reflective Observer

We need to keep in mind the effect that providing economically poor students with just twelve books of their own had on their feelings about themselves and their achievement in reading. Real, tangible things they can hold on to and use as reminders that we care about them and their literacy (McGill-Franzen, Allington, Yokoi, & Brooks, 1999).

. . . Our Collegial Teacher

The Alpha School provides all its Grade K–12 students with the latest laptop computers, including accessories for video calling. [In the real world, the state of Maine is well on the way to accomplishing this.] Students also receive smartphones on registration. Equipment is replaced regularly as better models become available, and backup files ensure that if a device is dropped, lost, or otherwise becomes useless, its information is replaced. And all students are taught to use devices and relevant applications by the teachers in the core subjects, all of whom have the latest equipment, know how to use it, and know how to teach their students to profit from devices and relevant software. Instruction for parents and other community members is available in the school, which is open from dawn to midnight and includes a branch of the public library. Programs like Infinite Campus bring school and home

> *close together. At this point in time, professional development supports the development and implementation of hybrid courses, support and assessment of distance/online study, and the study of student learning. A blend of teachers-supporting-teachers, distance support, and campus-based face-to-face support by experts makes up the menu. The school is a platform for professional development.*

This new century offers education a new world of digital possibilities—and considerable change has been happening. Some states have been providing laptops to all students at designated grade levels for many years (see, for example, Maine's Learning Technology Initiative, which provides computers for all students and teachers in Grades 7–12, www.maine.gov/mlti/index.shtml). Some rural school districts have initiated one-laptop programs to provide students and the community with greater access to each other and to global databases (see, for example, Greene County, North Carolina). Some school districts *are* beginning to supply laptops on registration. And some school districts are even mounting routers on school buses and turning them into "rolling study hall[s]" (Dillon, 2010).

This very day, more schools and classrooms are benefitting from the availability of ICT. Tomorrow more will embrace it. These changes are not driven by a massive governmental initiative, the implementation of a grand theory, pressure from lobbying organizations, or the initiatives of national organizations. ICT has grown and been disseminated throughout society with remarkable ease. Much of the public was ready and picked it up *naturally*.

Many energetic teachers and professional developers have been quick to incorporate education-related ICT applications into practice. However, much of the promise of ICT requires concerted efforts and systematic change. Pockets of excellence do not do the job. *All* students need top-quality education. That is, *all* need a first-class opportunity to learn. That said, technological innovations may be a key to addressing some long-deferred needs. In fact, we just might achieve equity this time around. America possesses a rich resource in its diversity, and public education has the potential to release the energy of historically underserved student populations to the benefit of all.

A revitalized core curriculum is another promise. If *that* promise is fulfilled, literacy in the society—that is for everybody—will be at a level only imagined a decade or so ago by the most optimistic futurists among us. Literacy—especially reading and writing—needs to be central in all curriculum areas to fulfill the promise of technology.

Our children are growing up in a world where their nursery is not only located in the home and neighborhood but also regularly interacts with the entire physical and social world. As they grow up, a provincial education will not suffice. Our children need home and school to become a joint academy that brings them smoothly into this rich, complex, multicultural planet. Media and information and communication technology enter the home, bearing wonderful gifts of images and ideas. In this context, the school needs to serve parents and other family members as well as the students. For example, communication between teachers and parents via email requires that the parents know how to use at least some computer programs. Thus, taking their places at the center of education are the promises of better capacity to inquire, enhanced skills to sort and warehouse knowledge, and the resolve to exercise moral purpose. And literacy, both the familiar varieties of reading and writing effectively and some new strains as well, will be at the center, enhanced by digital media. The individual, the family, the community, the nation, and the world will benefit in simultaneous cadence. What we call a *new literacy* will be born, one new in power and mobility.

We are on the way to use the changing culture as an impetus to make the educational improvements that we have needed to make for generations. We are ready

- to provide vastly higher levels of literacy than have been reached before.
- to make an inquiring, efficacious life a fundamental goal.
- to create a liberating state of equity that exceeds the loftiest ambitions of just a few years ago.

Enhancing the ancient home-school relationship—building a *real* partnership—will have a central role in fulfilling technological promise.

A transforming partnership between home and school promises that many distinctions between them will blur. Traditionally, we have seen the home as the nurturer/socializer and the school as the educator. Three changes are taking place:

1. Home and school are communicating and collaborating much more closely and regularly. A serious partnership is emerging. Parents are encouraged to become licensed paraprofessionals, and flexible scheduling and shared positions are becoming more common options.

2. More schooling is done on the home platform by both children and adults.

3. Parents are coming to the school more, not just on behalf of their children but as students themselves.

The promise of our time reaches far beyond the incorporation of ICT into school practice. Increasing intellectual capacity and moral judgment will be woven into the learning of content and skill. How to use knowledges and competencies in real life will be taught as they are acquired. The home-school partnership will transform. The promises are not just alluring visions but goals within our reach. ICT, applied to school renewal, makes the slope of change much less steep and slippery than it has been. However, while some changes will be easy, important ones will be hard. ICT will not just move in and make things better on its own. We will need to make serious use of our knowledge about how to make and sustain innovations.

THE NEW PROFESSION

A new genre of school improvement is promised as a significant part of teachers' work becomes formal and informal continuing education. Educators' lives will change radically as continuous learning pervades their teaching. Professional development will center on local *redeveloping* of courses and adapting units, strategies, and courses developed in other settings.

> *Our thesis:* A makeover of professional life enables and elevates the other promises. A new type of professional development—the learning life—will redesign the work of educators. Embracing our own new learning will be the key.

The evolving world demands a school where continuous inquiry by educators generates richer learning by students. Rather than teaching our current knowledge in the ways that we learned it, merely augmented by digital media, we will teach what we are learning in ways we are inventing. In the hands of educators, ICT itself will learn, as technology providers discover more needs of students and teachers and respond to them. We will stress often that an important work of teachers in the near term will be to build New Courses and adapt courses developed by others.

Authors' note: Our vision is evidence based. A large base of research supports our belief that conceptual, inquiry-centered approaches to curriculum and teaching generate high levels of student learning of information, concepts, and skills and produce positive movement toward learning and collaboration. Another line of research indicates that teachers can acquire and implement new skills easily, *provided* that appropriate professional development is available. See Chapter Twelve for reviews of some areas of the supporting research.

ACTUALIZING THE PROMISE: IMPLICATIONS

By now, our fellow 21st-century travelers are well acquainted with a variety of indirect effects of the spread of ICT specifically and electronic devices in general.

The list is long. Some are surprising, at least to those of us not in the technological industries. The proportion of people taking digital pictures and videos is amazing. The number of folks texting one another seems to increase exponentially every day. Governments are falling to uprisings fuelled by communications on Twitter.

Changes in commercial enterprises are startling. Go around the corner to buy a DVD or CD, and you wind up going home and ordering it on the Internet. The physical store, once part of a chain that was the darling of stock dealers, is now occupied by a seafood emporium featuring farm-raised creatures that have just been on a 5,000-mile journey toward our pots and grills. On a computer in the corner of the shop, you can place an order for live lobsters. DVD emporiums have come and gone. Our local store doesn't have our size in running shoes, but Joe's New Balance has every size online.

WHAT ABOUT EDUCATION?

We can expect some large effects, many unanticipated, on our educational institutions—effects that are not part of planned change on the part of those institutions.

There has been much talk about virtual schools and collections of online courses (piece by piece, you can create your own virtual school). The state of Florida's K–12 enrollment is more than 2.5 million students. Its Virtual School enrolls about 60,000 students. What this means is not yet clear, except that the virtual platform is enticing. Despite this trend, many of our ideas on the impact of distance learning on traditional educational institutions and professional categories are still speculation.

Let's think about the people and institutions that are vulnerable to change. *Vulnerable* is the operative word; here, this change may be a by-product of the big revolution. Changes may be thrust on the following practices—not with malicious intent but nonetheless a bit uncomfortable:

- Baccalaureate education
- Middle and high school education
- Preservice teacher education
- Lifelong professional development for educators at all levels

Baccalaureate Education

Bill Gates's recent suggestion (see Stross, 2011) that we identify the very best courses and morph them into distance offerings should make the faculty and administration of most colleges and universities shudder. Imagine a college curriculum with robust distance courses, complete with tutorial services and seminars (the last is technically the most difficult to create, but let's give innovators the benefit of the doubt). Imagine, in other words, a virtual baccalaureate college. This new institution is pulled together from a variety of sources (look for examples at offering from the Carnegie Mellon Open Learning Initiative and the New York Times Knowledge Network).

And look at the problems addressed by considering the virtual university as an option. To be sure, there is a loss in the social setting of college study. But at many residential colleges, students are taking more than four years to complete an undergraduate program; at many, in fact, half of the students *don't* finish. Moreover, in a virtual university, a dedicated student doesn't have to sit in class with an athlete who is paid to be there for reasons other than academic competence.

What happens to the professors as online universities evolve? How will their positions be affected? The answer is still unknown, but think about it. Will higher education departments primarily decide what distance courses will be offered in their catalog? Will professors take on the role of assistants to the leading professor-teachers in the nation?

Is this fantasy? Just consider that in the UK, more than 3 million students have graduated from the Open University, where courses are evaluated stringently (just write for a couple of days on topics that cover the lower and higher objectives) and, normally, have been gainfully employed while going to university.

Middle and High School Education

If the scenario above can happen in postsecondary education, might it not occur in secondary education? Again, develop great courses, create first-class tutorial options, and work out assessment procedures, and we have the virtual school. And a student can rush through the experience, graduate at 15, and get on with college. Or another student might lighten the load and take longer. The parents—or their children—can move to France for a year, and the student doesn't miss a beat.

Again, there is a loss of social milieu. But, that might not be all bad. In our little town, many parents ante up serious tuition money for a private school so their children can avoid the bullying that they believe is rampant in the public middle school. In many high schools, we have the phenomenon of the "empty senior year," which our current high schools have faced for 30 years and not solved. And the devastating overemphasis on competitive sports can be separated from academic activity. Imagine what a serious student thinks as his town builds a $50 million football stadium but declares the librarian must be cut because of budget shortfalls.

What happens to our current faculty members in this brave new world?

Preservice Teacher Education

The general objective is clear—to prepare teacher candidates to provide quality instruction for students and continue to learn throughout their careers. Can we redevelop teacher education with an emphasis on hybrid distance courses for preservice teacher candidates? And can technology bring the very best professors of the core subjects—particularly reading, writing, and arithmetic—to campuses while local professors provide hands-on training in the core education subjects?

Lifelong Professional Development for Educators at All Levels

School systems could become, as Bob Schaefer put it many years ago, "schools as centers of inquiry," where educators are collaborative teacher-researchers. In this role, they continually build hybrid environments where face-to-face campus interactions and distance resources are integrated so as to improve the education of students.

EQUITY AND OPPORTUNITY

If all students are brought into the ICT world and taught to inquire, achievement by all students should rise, and equity across our educational systems should increase dramatically. The gaps should close. Some private schools have already gotten the message. Consider the advertisements for the "Avenues World School—one of the first global schools serving children from 3 to 18." This school is planned to open in New York City in 2012, and campuses are planned in China, India, and 18 other countries. "They will graduate with advanced fluency in a second language, have the opportunity to study at several campuses around the world, all part of one school (the curriculums in each will be consistent with one another) and experience a 15-year global studies curriculum created by leading university scholars." The tuition will be at the level of the other private schools in Manhattan—around US$35,000 per year (Avenues, n.d.).

Such a school is within our technical capability. The issue raised now is whether *all* children will have the opportunities promised by Avenues and its counterparts (with the exception of adjunct foreign travel because of logistical issues—imagine 4 million American students and 80 million students from other countries physically travelling back and forth).

However, the equity issue is now joined. The famous American private schools have always conferred huge advantages on their students. Now American suburban schools and rural schools can catch up as can, finally, schools serving our most impoverished urban kids.

5 Platforms for Education

The Enhanced School/Home Educational System

SCENES

CHARLIE

Fifteen-year-old Charlie is perched on a high stool in front of a shelf he has made to hold his computer, accessories, and three or four open books. Above the shelf is a bookcase on whose shelves sit a number of potted plants, labeled according to treatments.

Charlie is taking a BSCS-based Advanced Placement course, an online distance offering by a state university. He lives in a small Georgia town and goes to a high school that serves about 75 students in each grade. Last summer the biology teacher resigned for personal reasons, and the district officials have not yet found a suitable replacement. Thus, Charlie is taking the distance course. The district has not yet decided whether to accept distance courses for credit, so Charlie is taking it for college credit, which, if necessary, he can transfer to the school.

The potted plants are part of his course-related project. Tomato plants in his family's vegetable garden have not been healthy or yielding well. He is experimenting with a number of variables—soil, fertilizer, water—in an attempt to find an optimal mix. The plants currently on his shelf migrate to other environments—an ultraviolight center, the center of a fountain ... Charlie's room has become a platform on which he seeks learning.

We will meet our enterprising Charlie later.

NANCY OLSON

Nancy's pleasant home has a number of fine attributes and one really distinctive feature—her inquiry center. As in many American households, family life centers around the eat-in kitchen center and the family room, where a fireplace and entertainment center, comfy sofas and chairs, plush carpet, and pillows welcome the kids and parents and visitors.

The "living" room in many houses has become a bit extraneous. When she and her husband looked for a house, Nancy lobbied for a big kitchen with room for a big dining table. And she lobbied for an outsized family room connected to the kitchen.

She is constantly involved in inquiries using books and online resources. But she likes to be near her family rather than in a separated space in the spare room upstairs. So Nancy converted the often unused "living room" into her learning and work space platform. Print books fill the shelves on one wall. In the center is a big old Victorian oak table where her computers, monitors, video equipment, and printers hold sway.

Nancy Olson is a high school science teacher. As we look into her world, she is, like Charlie, studying BSCS materials with resources provided online by another state university. She and her colleague, Judy, are revamping their science offerings. Part of their motivation for studying at a distance is to better understand the potential of online and distance offerings for the students in their school. Thus, they are both strengthening their campus courses and preparing the way for their students to learn from a combination of face-to-face and distance modes; essentially, they are developing a set of hybrid courses.

A side effect of their interests and development of the family's uses of technology is that their children have become ICT literate. They are beginning to ask whether they can take certain distance courses. The family is edging toward occupying a summer with some travel as well as a period when some time most days is occupied with distance inquiry or course taking.

Nancy and Judy will also look in on us later.

MARY BISHOP

Mary's sixth-grade classroom is inhabited by more than 1,000 fiction and nonfiction books. This third week of October, she is focusing the students on styles to use when selecting titles for narrative pieces. She has selected 30 books, and, using the covers, the students are classifying their titles. When they have built a number of categories, they will practice generating some stories of their own, emulating the styles of the published authors.

In this unit, the print medium is central. When writing, the students will use their laptops and networked printers, and they will read and respond to each other's work on their class blog. However, her course does not begin in cyberspace; online resources aren't introduced until students begin to access newspapers and libraries and extend their categories.

Without strong literacy skills, students cannot profit from the cyberspace revolution. Mary epitomizes the kind of teacher who is essential if the promise is to be fulfilled. She begins with the inductive activity, using the print library, and then accesses web-based sources. Another hybrid environment is created, one that begins face-to-face and then increasingly uses the New Libraries.

Mary will also visit us later as we develop our theme.

TOM AND THE COUNTRIES OF THE WORLD

Tom's yearlong course, for students from Grade 9 through Grade 12, provides a foundation for global understanding. This year his students have begun studying the 20 countries he has selected. The students classify countries on demographic variables, using databases such as the excellent World Factbook produced by the CIA. Then they examine the webpages belonging to cities in those countries. Their first task is to develop hypotheses about relationships among variables in the databases, for example, "Is GNP or GDP related to fertility?"

As the students learn about apparent statistical relationships within the 20 countries, they will expand their inquiry, selecting other countries in order to test their hypotheses. They will also try to find authorities—specialists in these areas—and talk with them on-site, live via Skype, or via email.

Tom represents schooling where information and communication technology enhance campus-based courses in the core curriculum areas. Face-to-face, campus-based seminars are supported by the New Libraries. Like the others, he will look in on us again as we explore that dimension of our inquiry—the creation of hybrid schools.

ANN ESPINOSA

Ann Espinosa, striving for yet another way to help her tenth-grade students achieve global literacy, introduced them to the online newspapers database. When we last checked, hundreds of newspapers from 80 countries were available. (As an aside, we found this same database to be accessible in an internationally oriented bookstore on a laptop set up for its patrons.) Ann announced that she was giving students two or three questions and then they were to generate some of their own—to be sorted out to focus further inquiries.

First, she asked students to find out how many of the 80 countries (aside from the United States) had an English-language newspaper in the database. They then mapped the countries according to which did and did not have one, seeking to learn whether they were clustered regionally. Second, since it was World Cup season, she asked the students to learn how many of the countries' newspapers, regardless of language, covered the World Cup soccer games and also reported baseball standings. Much discussion ensued. The students concluded that World Cup soccer matches were being reported virtually everywhere, but baseball was reported in just a few countries. Students speculated on the reasons for the difference. Third, she asked the students to learn how certain events were described in the English-language newspapers of the countries where languages other than English were the most common.

Authors' note: In our workshops and courses, we and our close colleagues have been using the global-information databases for 25 years. Our students now have direct access to information (and people) from cities, towns, and countries around the globe—a major ICT innovation. The venerable pen pal has come of age with a vengeance, and the occasional well-traveled visitor to the classroom is augmented or replaced with information from the source countries. Consult the publications *Social Education* and *Social Studies for the Young Learner* to enjoy the richness of print and digital materials that comprise the New Library for the social studies.

The Young Lady From Iran

The young woman seated next to us at the sushi bar exuded a vaguely exotic air; her looks and style, we thought, made it likely that she was not American.

But then she spoke in perfect American English, even ending her declarative sentences in that rising lilt of many young Californians.

As it turns out, however, she wasn't from these parts after all; she was born in Iran and spoke only Farsi until her arrival here two years ago. What classes, we wondered, had she attended to learn the language so well?

"I didn't," she said. "I used Rosetta Stone."

Source: Taub, E. A. (2010, February 27). The Web way to learn a language. *The New York Times.*

The source of this excerpt—from a recent *New York Times* article—goes on to discuss various language programs on DVDs and online and sometimes with combinations of contact with native speakers and instructors. Our Young Lady From Iran epitomizes the degree to which skill in self-education will determine the futures of our global citizens—folks who are growing up literally everywhere. Importantly, when we study with packages of materials, the environment feels much like a distance course without provision for contact with an instructor.

WINDOWS ON THE WORLD

Charlie, Nancy, Mary, Tom, Ann, and the Young Lady From Iran use their environments as platforms from which they access learning opportunities.

Homes and schools are windows on the world and always have been. Not only do they teach and acculturate, but they help us peek out beyond our immediate surroundings. School curricula have given us a place to begin to develop tools for inquiring when school days are over. For generations, the school library has gifted us immeasurably. At the same time, the home is a laboratory where we practice inquiring, socializing, and loving. And the home takes us beyond its boundaries and leads us down the street to the churches and stores and sights that are somewhere out there.

What has changed is that technology has enabled us to journey beyond our homes, neighborhoods, and schools in a way that our ancestors could never have imagined. And these cybervoyages provide opportunities for unprecedented learning. Before about 1880, the outside world came into home and school in the accounts of travelers who had crossed borders and through books, magazines, and newspapers. By the mid-1700s, those avenues provided a considerable number of self-teaching opportunities. We have always been impressed that, by the time they were 25 years old, Hamilton, Madison, and Jefferson had read *everything in print in the English language*. They approached the drafting of the Constitution with the print part of the culture in their heads! Printed text gave them their windows on the world.

Since their time, not only has print media exploded in quantity and diversity, but the development of new technologies has opened new and powerful avenues between the larger world and home and school. These trails have been constructed by the telephone, phonograph, radio, television, computer, and mobile devices. In the process, they have been broadened, paved digitally, and turned into boulevards with two-way traffic. Now school and home are not just recipients but interactive entities—parts of the Big World in their own right. As this paragraph is being written, a terrible crisis in Haiti has resulted in a call for donations by the Red Cross. More than $200 million has been pledged in the past week, with $21 million raised through a texting initiative! As part of the effort, a group of 20 nine- and ten-year-olds raised their contribution in the old-fashioned way. They set up a hot cocoa stand in their neighborhood and sold enough to send a $1,300 check to the Red Cross. Stories like these will be legion by the time this book is in your hands. The social media are having a very large impact on a great many people. Some governments should be very nervous when they consider how easily protests and even insurrections can be organized today.

Steadily, home and school have evolved into what we can now see are platforms for learning. From them we can access information, receive instruction, and communicate. These platforms are not being fully utilized as yet, but considerable change has already happened in many homes and schools and the potential is enormous. New learning has affected many ordinary happenings.

> *Authors' note:* The other day we realized that we have attended three weddings in the last three years where one party was a member of our family or a close friend—very traditional. What is not so customary is that two of the new couples met in cyberspace. One pair lived on different continents and met on an online motorcycle club. (Did we say "motorcycle club"?) The second pair lived a short distance away from each other but would not have crossed paths in person; instead, they met online. The third pair met by smiling at each other in a restaurant. That noted, they gathered the small wedding party in a lovely setting in another country—a setting that they had found perched in cyberspace.
>
> You can't help wondering what paths their lives would have taken BICT (before ICT).

In these homely examples, the new partners *learned*, the members of the wedding parties *learned*, and a circle of friends *learned*. Among the new knowledge was awareness of the force of new ways of making friends and becoming lovers. The new partners were explorers. Our home, our family, was the intimate setting—a new platform floating in its own corner of cyberspace.

THE THREE BIG CHANGES
(THUS FAR) FOR EDUCATION

Of the changes that are morphing home and school into platforms for learning, three stand out.

1. *The New Library:* We now have access to unprecedented amounts of information, 24 hours a day, through what we have deemed the New Library. Growing as if by magic, a massive database has appeared on the doorstep of every school and home. Not long from now, many of the world's libraries will be linked together, making what is oftened termed the *universal library.*

2. *Distance resources and New Courses:* Resource-based distance education is coming of age. New formal and informal instructional opportunities are appearing and maturing. ICT is spawning new institutions and changing old ones into cyberplaces where you can find a huge range of courses and curriculums. The New Course is with us in two forms—the stand-alone DVD-mail-fax-email-online variety and as part of virtual schools where it is a part of the curriculum, also using a variety of modes of communication.

3. *New communication tools:* Interactive communication devices and Web 2.0 applications are cross-breeding at an expanding rate, increasing one's ability to enter other environments, draw from them, and even act on them. Just about the time you learn to use your cell phone, you have to welcome the next generation of smarter phones. Just about time you get comfortable with wikis and blogs, along comes Jing. Just as you get comfortable with Skype and Adobe Connect, you need to work with colleagues who prefer GoToMeeting. New habits are springing up along with these new communication tools, and new quandaries are rising. A student recently asserted that he preferred reading electronic books on his smartphone because he could text as he read! Fat chance, but he certainly can switch back and forth. The really big changes are being brought about by the newly developing virtual schools, which we will discuss in the next chapter.

Let's look at our reconstituted platforms and consider how our New Libraries, distance learning and New Courses, and new communication tools fit into them.

The New Libraries

We don't need to enumerate here all the positive features of the process of inquiry using Google and its siblings. Websites, articles in Wikipedia, maps of everywhere, scientific studies—vast amounts of informed and off-the-wall opinion—await our queries. Our cell phones whiz us into outsized informational warehouses staffed by sophisticated cyberassistants. And we need to remember that more and more of the holdings of conventional libraries and museums are now lined up in these new electronic warehouses. The Library of Congress (www.loc.gov/) and the libraries of our greatest universities and cities are just a click away (e.g., http://digitalcollections.harvard.edu/; http://digitalcollections.library .yale.edu/; http://library.duke.edu/digitalcollections/). Whenever Emily is working on a photo data set for inductive lessons, it's hard to get her away from the Library of Congress—on her computer.

Distance Learning

A massive set of information resources and online courses provide unlimited opportunities for self-education. And, because of that, online homeschooling is getting wheels. Federal statistics show about 3 percent of American children (1.5 million) are now homeschooled. Reasons for this choice vary: About 40 percent do so for religious reasons, about 20 percent for fear of bullying and other unpleasant aspects of the school social environment, and about 10 percent because of concerns about instructional quality.

There used to be a saying that your neighborhood school taught all the kids the same stuff, but their homes differed greatly in the amount and quality of what was learned there and that was why everybody did not finish at the same place. The coming of ICT can exacerbate those differences hugely. Conversely, the leveling of the playing field has never been more within reach. A recent study by the Kaiser Family Foundation indicated that the average American schoolchild spends about 7.5 hours per day using some form of electronic media or device—an increase from 6.5 five years ago (Lewin, 2010). Significantly, media often fills what would have otherwise been "dead time." While waiting in the car for their parents to conclude an errand, children listen to music, speak to their friends, take and send pictures, receive and send text, write and search with their laptops, and read ebooks. Many of their parents—and their grandparents, the Baby Boomers, who are beginning to retire—have lived their entire adult lives in a post-Walkman world; they cannot remember a time when libraries of music did not accompany them.

The Kaiser study did not include adults, but at work and at home, the amount of time we spend connected to electronic media is remarkable. Complaints about today's television offerings are legion, but we are more impressed by opportunities to learn than by the schlock. Today, the Turner Classic Movies channel announced that, leading up to the Academy Awards, it would show outstanding films from the beginning of talkies to now—93 fine movies in all, 3 a night. The history of film is there to be enjoyed—and to be studied in courses on the literature of film. Foreign films are being imported again but courtesy of Netflix and colleagues, not the multiplex.

We are continually amazed by the increased opportunities for learning and tools for teaching thanks to developments in ICT. A good many sensible and tested educational alternatives, fuelled by huge government grants, have failed to achieve the degree of implementation now happening in concert with the socio-technical change in the larger society—happening organically, not by mandate.

Learning how to use the New Libraries effectively, whether to support the learning of students or our own professional development, is critical and becoming more so by the minute. How to develop questions, search for relevant material, organize it once it is found, and draw conclusions and take actions. . . . Learning how to learn has jumped to the head of the educational objectives list. Aside from quantity of sources, the convenience of cyber-entrée to information provides enormous advantages compared to the access to and offerings of the best libraries only a few years ago.

New Courses

The cyberspace school grows apace. Resource-based educational opportunities—self-education through the use of structured materials—have been growing since the days of the correspondence school and mail-order offerings. There have been some dramatic jumps in the past, as in the development of the General Educational Development (GED) test, the advent of the Open University in the UK, and the assembly of multimedia packages. *Sesame Street* recently celebrated its 50th birthday. More quietly than the New Library rose up around us, the *new school* is creating itself.

In a course, instructional materials or instructors lead the student through activities designed to build certain kinds of knowledge and skill. The term *curriculum* derives from the Roman word for "course" in the sense of a closed track, generally round or oval, although it can be linear as in cross-country or marathon racing. Courses can be very highly structured or can use sets of inductive or problem-solving exercises. Use of the library can be an integral part of them. We now have campus-based, home-based, distance-based, and hybrid courses playing in an improvised concert with one another. We need to remind ourselves regularly that print media—books included—are still valuable resources. In the hands of a skilled reader, books have been the most powerful self-instructional system society has known to date, and books have been the base for learning in unexpected areas. Any tennis fan knows the story of Richard Williams reading a book about the sport and teaching Venus and Serena to do a lot more than have a few rallies on Sunday afternoons.

Aside from several million books, an enormous number of resource-based courses are currently available that use several media and transmit their content electronically. A significant number are of very high quality; for example, most of those in the New York Times Knowledge Network take us to sophisticated shores previously reached only by swimming the Hudson.

The offerings relevant to elementary and secondary education include variations of the common core subjects and a much larger range of other content than the staff of any physical school site could possibly offer. Many educators have been skeptical about the effectiveness of these online offerings compared to face-to-face instruction. We will not summarize the relevant research here except to comment that many students learn quite well from a considerable range of courses. Neither the straightforward text-and-talk variety nor the inquiry-oriented variety should be dismissed out of hand. A fine review by Clardy (2009) provides a balanced description of the literature that should, at the least, alleviate some of the concerns that are raised. We will cover the research bases in our final chapter.

> As school and home are melded into new partnerships and communities are more involved in education, new governance structures are needed for schools. We recommend the development of what we call the Responsible Parties, an expanded governance structure involving faculty, community members, and others. See especially Chapters Six and Eleven for discussions of membership and process.

As time passes, more and better distance courses, many online, will become available. And large numbers of our students will take them. We need to ensure that the school is a good platform for them and that homes are supported as they, too, become platforms for distance learning. The virtual schools that offer K–12 courses in a package can inspire a vision of actually replacing the school as we have known it.

PROOFS OF EFFECTIVENESS

In Chapter Twelve, we will provide information about currently available studies that address how the incorporation of ICT may affect educational outcomes. Much work is needed, but there is a good basis of documented success with distance education initiatives on which we can build. The important issue is whether various forms of distance education can do the job they are designed for rather than whether they can do it better than a given customary practice. For example, the establishment and availability of broadcast television led to two parallel innovations that have had an enormous influence on, in the first case, the social system in the United Kingdom and, in the second, increased opportunities for learning at home—particularly in the United States.

In 1969, The Open University was established in the UK. It was "open" in two senses. First, any high school graduate could enroll. Second, instruction was delivered largely through distance means, although supplementary tutorial centers were established throughout the country. More than 3 million students have attended. Most work as full-time employees (many employers support students with time and money), and the average student graduates within about six years. Achievement is monitored rigorously—within the tradition of the most prominent British universities—and an enormous range of courses is offered. BBC broadcasts were prominent in the courses until a few years ago, when the spread of DVD players was wide enough that the broadcasts could be discontinued. Only five years after the institution's inception, the number of students graduating from university in the UK had doubled, and the rate has gradually increased. At this time, the number of citizens with university degrees is well over twice what would have been the case had The Open University not been established.

Sesame Street is the second major distance education institution we are referring to. For 50 years, millions of students have studied its offerings, which include not only learning in literacy but also in social skills and civil manners.

Both of these massive innovations offer what was not possible before new media. We believe that the innovations generated by imaginative adaptations of ICT will have an accelerating impact on education, both formal and informal.

COMPARISONS: DISTANCE VERSUS CAMPUS

However, everywhere we go, people ask how well distance courses compare with campus courses. We are less often asked how ICT can enhance campus courses, but we believe that hybrid courses will turn out to be richer and more effective than past campus courses have generally been—and some of them are truly excellent.

A straightforward way to think comparatively about learning from campus and distance courses is that generally equivalent (in content and process) courses generate similar amounts of learning in each venue (see reviews by Bernard et al., 2004; Zhao et al., 2005). In both cases, students vary in what they learn, but the variance is similar. Also, both campus and distance courses display considerable variance in effectiveness. Imagine a textbook-centered Introduction to Algebra. Mean achievement is similar, but achievement is also very uneven. The good news is that most students can learn how to learn from both campus and distance versions of a course, but the bad news is that there are poor, average, and above-average courses of each type.

Comparing campus and distance courses covering the same content is the most conservative way of estimating what ICT can bring. We envision capitalizing on the technologies by developing inquiry-oriented courses—on and off campus—that take advantage of technology and also are based on the proven value of inductive curriculum and instruction. We know how to build outstanding courses of both types.

Postsecondary education has been a good address for resource-based courses with content both familiar and unfamiliar. As we mentioned earlier, The Open University in the UK has had outstanding results across the spectrum of university courses from freshman through senior years for more than 40 years. The development of the New Courses combines with the New Library to present a situation where a large part of the core education of many students in, say, Grade 4 through college graduation can be accomplished effectively through hybrid courses that capitalize on the best of both worlds.

Energetic teachers are already developing hybrid courses, and, in some cases, schools are managing an infusion of technology throughout the curriculum. We are not far from being able to assemble cyberschools. (We are not referring to the widely advertised commercially developed variety.) American colleges and universities are offering considerable numbers of distance courses. Some private entrepreneurial universities are now advertising entire programs and even curricula in clinical areas, such as teaching. Imagine online preservice teacher education. Hybrids are probably a better option in clinical and performance areas like teaching, but a great deal of entrepreneurial and technical imagination is tackling the possibilities. Essentially, the *virtual* school has become a *reality*. Virtual schools will have their place, though of course not all will pay off for students.

Accessibility is an attractive aspect of online learning. Just a few years ago, if folks where we live in Georgia wanted graduate study, they had to drive several hundred miles to attend courses. Today . . . you all know the picture. If we had our way, everybody would have a laptop or an equivalent device—and better and better ones will be designed and built. But they need to be accessible to everyone. *Everyone.*

COMMUNICATION DEVICES AND BASIC APPLICATION SOFTWARE ("APPS")

Without the physical devices and software needed to access them, the New Library and New Courses would not exist. Imagine a student's room being furnished with an iPod, a Droid, a laptop, a satellite video connection, a wall of bookshelves, a desk, a couple of very comfortable chairs, and a bed.

Some of the devices and their basic applications have had an enormous impact on living, interacting, and working and have enlarged the places where electronic activity can take place. The accessibility of mobile devices has had a massive impact on use of ICT. A major equity question will be whether we invest, probably through schools, to provide all students with what they need to take advantage of this new world. Our response: Most emphatically, we *must*! The equipment for Charlie's room should be supplied when he registers for school. Nancy's equipment needs to be delivered to her on her first day on the job.

Just writing about these possibilities—and what has already taken place—makes us proud and excited about the future.

But, education is an animal inhabited by some old habits that have enabled it to escape some very promising innovations.

ISSUES AND DISTRACTIONS

Perennials and New Shoots

The promise of our times renews some old questions and raises some new ones. The following two will receive continuous attention in this book and will require attention in the coming years. They call out for serious inquiry, will not be resolved quickly or casually, and will not creep quietly away on their own.

> *What has to be taught by a face-to-face teacher, and what can a student learn as well through independent inquiry?*

This old, unresolved question is sharply redefined by the application of information and communication technology to education. No simple answer will emerge. How well students learn to teach themselves will be a major factor. Both children and adults have tremendous individual differences in this area. (Imagine how Jefferson and Hamilton stood out in terms of their self-educating capacity.) Schooling can affect those differences. We *can* help people learn how to learn. Within schools, as we will see, the hybrid course is probably the next logical stage of development. But good self-educators have always roared ahead, and they now have afterburners.

The important question is not whether instructor-led classes, hybrids, or distance offerings are the best choices for all purposes. Rather the focus of our inquiry must be what is the best mix for a given school. Good learning can take place with all options. However, the school as a platform needs to be a vibrant society. The effects of both campus and distance courses are partly determined by the synergy of school and home and the vitality of their partnership.

Literacy skills will continue to be central to learning. Ironically, the emergence of the ITC complex may finally drive us to provide the level of literacy instruction that has been needed for so long. The ancient adage of building schooling on readin,' writin,' and 'rithmetic has a new urgency today. Without literacy, there is so much more to lose in today's world.

Schools and homes are now both viable platforms for learning. The school is a very important center of the neighborhood and town. But the home has greater maneuverability. Developing access to distance courses provides a good example. If the biology department of a high school decides it would like to increase access to a distance provider, educators must work through layers of decision makers and may have to achieve consensus from the rest of the faculty. The family can simply call up and register.

If you want to start a movement in your community, you can do so more easily from home. That is one of the reasons that charter schools are so popular. They entice us to "just do it." But most current charter (and virtual) schools are depressingly ordinary. We need to find out how to bring the maneuverability of the home to the business of collective education.

Cautions About Our "Fix-It" Faith

The obvious enhancements to human capacity are pretty well accepted by most folks, with the usual grumbling about possible problems and scary swamps, but a nice article in the *New York Times* suggested that we may have developed a general belief that technologies will rise to every occasion (Rosenthal, 2010). The author begins by citing a talk given in 2005 by the vice president for BP's deepwater developments in the Gulf of Mexico in which he said that deepwater exploration will bring *surprises* and we will find that we're not quite ready to respond to some of them. Just a bit prophetic, eh?

However, Rosenthal (2010) does not use this prophecy to add to the laments and litanies of the real problems of the Gulf oil spill. She uses it to illuminate our drift into a fix-it faith—"an unswerving belief that technology will save us—it is the cavalry coming over the hill, just as we are about to lose the battle." And many good experiences support our belief. She mentions, among other things, the Green Revolution and the extent to which vaccines have virtually eradicated many children's diseases. In addition, medical technology battles AIDS. Contraceptives fight over-population and lower the incidence of unwanted pregnancies (which many experts believe will be the basic solution to the cycles of poverty that plague the United States). If one becomes too sanguine that adding digital components to education will improve learning, one can neglect other components, such as instruction in reading and writing, that are critical. The huge proportion of students who drop out of high school—20 to 60 percent, depending on the socioeconomic status of the district—may not be saved by digital technologies alone.

A Worthwhile Caution

We are reminded of Federal Reserve chair Alan Greenspan's comments that "irrational exuberance" was driving Wall Street throughout the last decade. We are in no such danger of that in education. We do have sound evidence that we can use technology to improve education. But to limit ourselves to a model that is fueled only by technology and to eschew the increments of progress we can make through plain hard work would be a significant mistake.

Potential Collateral Liabilities

It is not surprising that some observers worry that social networking can become a substitute for face-to-face friendship. Hopefully some schol-arly attention will be directed toward fact-finding in this area. Digital com-munication is not immune to excesses, as we are reminded by this interesting column where Maureen Dowd's title tells it all: "Are Cells the New Cigarettes?" (2010). Dowd is not talking about cells or cigarettes as carcinogens. Rather, she is referring to the habitual, compulsive use of cell phones as an example of technology as a "narcotic."

THE EVOLVING HIGH SCHOOL

In Chapter Nine we give considerable attention to a crossroads under-lined in an excellent article by Coughlin (2010), which cautions us that secondary schools could easily drift into credentialing institutions as students increasingly present online courses as substitutes for the cam-pus variety. Alternatively, the high school can remake itself, in the pro-cess working to solve problems like the dissolving senior year, the worrisome graduation rates (and competence of many graduates), and the increasing division of the student body into athletic team squads and the "others." In some high schools, virtually the only full-time seniors are sports team members. A frightening proportion of the "others" are just taking a course or two to finish graduation requirements and hanging out. As virtual schools become more widespread, the high school as we have known it is likely to change. And school districts are developing their own virtual schools that can offer digital alternatives to the whole curriculum.

PROFESSIONAL DEVELOPMENT ONLINE

Professional development is a very humble example of the changes that are coming. Not long ago, nearly all professional development was led by an instructor or was done through self-instruction by groups of teachers—such as professional learning communities. Today on this desk are catalogs listing 78 online courses from the Association for Supervision and Curriculum Development, 100 from public broadcasting, and 20 from each of a half dozen consulting firms. Unfortunately, many of these offerings are replicas of the much-criticized brief workshops. Fascinating are advertisements from universities—some venerable, others new inventions of convenience—offering preservice education and master's degrees in various specialties. At first blush, these ads are shocking: How on earth can a clinical field like education be trained entirely through distance means? On the other hand, many universities have essentially outsourced clinical practice to schools and cooperating teachers and supervise them casually.

With respect to distance professional development, Emily has some favorites, as do some of you. But overall, we have much to do to help these courses live up to their promises. Much research and development are needed.

Some of the changes in our world have a funny side to them.

Authors' note: The first draft of the above paragraph was taking shape during a vacation. We were carefully measuring out the time we allot to email traffic and writing each day. The lady in the hotel room next door had a daily 4:30 PM appointment over Skype with her two cats. Did we say *cats?* Cyberspace entertains her retirement days while we, a few feet away, paddle to keep up while striving to prevent our new technologies from eroding our holiday by overwhelming us with waves of "urgent" messages.

Let's close this chapter on that note.

6

The 21st-Century Skills

WILLIAM LODERMEIER'S TECHNOLOGY EDUCATION LAB

Curriculum and instruction in technology education have changed dramatically in the last 30 years, and ICT has been incorporated extensively in both process and content. The International Technology and Engineering Educators Association (ITEEA) developed standards for technological literacy—the general education needed by everyone—for all students. Professional technology educators like William Lodermeier have taken those standards seriously and developed or adopted course materials. Emily was fortunate enough to visit Willie's classroom in an Ames (Iowa) Middle School and learned about the curriculum and how Willie uses it in the eighth grade. The classroom includes 16 workstations, the teacher's workstation, and an area where the whole class can assemble for teacher-led sessions.

Ames Middle School operates on a 12-week trimester schedule, and the technology course is offered five times each trimester. During the eighth grade, the students rotate among the technology course, an art course, and a family and consumer science course (evolved from home economics), taking all three by the end of the year.

Willie adopted and adapted a software-based, self-instructional curriculum developed by LJ Create. The LJ course package includes the student computers, each of which contains the software for one of the 16 modules that are offered. The teacher's computer is networked to the others, so Willie can look at the students' work via computer to see what they are doing and whether they need help.

Each module is designed for ten hours of instruction (two weeks of classroom time). Willie's classes enroll between 22 and 30 students. Nearly all have the Microsoft Office Suite under their belts. With some help from Willie, the students organize themselves into groups of two, and the pairs state their preferences for the topics covered by the modules. Willie tries to accommodate those preferences as he assigns them to the computers. The modules include Digital Photography, Graphics and Animation, Robotics and Animation, Basic Electricity, Electronic Communications, and Automotive Technology.

During the first seven sessions of the course, Willie uses a combination of lectures and demonstrations to introduce the class to the course materials and structure and to the necessary vocabulary. He then shows the students how to get started and moves from station to station, facilitating and scaffolding students' experiences, helping them to teach themselves. A few students may need extra help, and he is there to provide it. Although designed for approximately ten hours each, these modules are self-paced. Some students proceed quickly and begin another module earlier than the average. However, the modules offer gateways to further study, and some students become interested in the material and may occupy many hours beyond the basic ten. An example is the module on animation, which offers many possibilities for further study and intrigues some of the students in most classes.

Competency measures are embedded in the software program. Willie uses the results to have students "reteach" themselves when needed, and he converts the results into grades for the course. Over the years, he has modified some of the written assignments and added others, and these assignments are graded and the scores combined with the measures embedded in the software. Every three weeks, information about progress is posted on the Infinite Campus where both students and parents can see it. Each student and parent has a user name and password used to access progress and assignments. Essentially, this is a teaching and grade book management platform that serves Willie, students, parents, and school record keeping. Willie can look at a student's history if he needs to.

Here we have a fine example of a software-based course in the hands of a professional technology educator who has adopted a curriculum that provides a solid base for instruction in skill with, understanding of, and an appreciation of technological literacy. Willie wants students to apply their skills and understandings in their future lives. For example, most will have access to an automobile sometime in the next few years. They need to practice preventive maintenance to avoid expensive repairs. And, when they need repairs, they need to be able to inquire into options, costs, and the like.

Technological literacy is to be both learned and applied.

Inductive inquiry—individual and collective—is the centerpiece. Many laypeople and educators were brought up to believe that learning and thinking capacities are genetic traits that we are born with. Some of us were also led to believe that these capacities are relatively immune to the influences of environment, whether home or school. We now understand that learning how to learn, how to collect and organize data, and how to live an inquiring life can be learned *after* birth. Good platforms provide jumping-off places for our beloved and valuable children. For all practical purposes, intelligence can be learned. And, therefore, it can be taught if we make intelligence-producing environments our business in home and school.

The 21st-century skills are essentially an updated version of the belief that education can actually make a big difference to the quality of life that our children will have, some from increased capacity but much coming from social contribution, near and far.

. . . Our Reflective Observer

At first, when people began talking about 21st-century skills, I thought I had been left behind somehow. Then I discovered that they were not off-the-wall but actually on my wall. I could use the digital revolution to make my courses better and better by using the New Libraries and new distance offerings. And it was all within reach. The cybertools are a big help. But we teachers will do the work of building curriculum and teaching students how to learn.

. . . Our Collegial Teacher

Nurturing the ability to learn may be more important than just teaching the obviously relevant ICT skills. The digital world is changing rapidly. Programs, processes, and devices spill into our world of learning continuously; thus, teaching students how to learn and solve problems takes precedence over the teaching of any particular program or technological tool. My university students often want me to teach them tools. I teach them skills, and then they can choose their tools.

. . . Our University Colleague

Students learn skills by seeing them, understanding them, and practicing them until they become an integrated part of the students' repertoire. Thus, the models of teaching that fit the requirements of our time are in the inductive, cooperative, and inquiry-complex.

. . . The Authors

Educators, business leaders, and concerned citizens have organized and presented school districts, states, and the federal government with suggested priorities for curriculum and instruction in America's schools. The movement initiated and supported by the National Governors Association (NGA) and the Council of Chief State School Officers (CCSSO) to have states adopt the same core curriculum standards in literacy and mathematics has been amazingly successful. However, we worry that the Common Core State Standards have not made learning how to learn and to apply knowledge and thinking skills as prominent as we think they should be. The new standards should not be dominated by a somewhat retro view of education. However, the developers of the Standards are clear in their purpose: "to provide a clear and consistent framework to prepare our children for college and the workforce" (www.corestandards .org/about-the-standards/). The Partnership for 21st Century Skills is making a serious effort to create a focused vision of high-priority skills and to persuade states, professional organizations, and large districts to adopt its conception of skills as part of the core objectives of education. The skills advocated by the Partnership are a useful addition to the Common Core. While both these initiatives promote a standard base for a national curriculum in literacy, mathematics, and the application of technology, we must be careful that they do not limit the learning opportunities and curriculum experiences we provide our children.

In this chapter, we examine the Partnership's view of 21st-century skills and tie them to knowledge about teaching strategies that can achieve them and knowledge about how teachers learn. The Partnership advocates important skills, and we understand the models of curriculum and teaching that can bring them to reality—what teachers need to do to move from present practice to the world of blended and hybrid courses. We try to understand how past history of the use of media in education can inform our efforts today as we adapt existing models of professional development to implement the emerging ones. The digital skills that educators need to make desirable changes *now* are well within reach with Web 2.0 tools.

Authors' note: Without social and moral intelligence, "just doing" is empty. Technologies enhance some of our capabilities, and we should put them to work. But when we reflect on how the banks and investment companies used their new tools to create derivatives, pull off scams, and just plain magnify a variety of bad judgments, we can see that our Dark Side can be enhanced as well as our most moral and responsible side. We need each other as companions on a great journey, not as entities to be exploited impersonally.

We need to remember that technological achievements are brought about by people with true grit and determination who drive themselves to a state of excellent knowledge. They work hard at the job and at the preparation to do it. A can-do-it spirit has great merit, as does the old slogan "When the going gets tough, the tough get going," which was the mantra of the World War II Seabees. In our current world, having the grit to see an unpopular vision into reality is very important. The creators of the personal computer, the Internet, the browsers, the personal video players . . . all ran upstream against terrific odds.

We need focused energy to bring America's schools to the levels that our children deserve. Waiting passively for technology to get the job done is no longer a viable option. Fewer schools than should are presently using technology schoolwide as an integral part of instruction or as a tool to support students' individual and collective learning. The extra effort to change curriculum, instruction, and, very important, the social climate of schools will be what fulfills the promises.

THE 21ST-CENTURY PARTNERSHIP: POLITICAL ACTION AND REAL POSSIBILITIES

A well-funded and politically astute movement was developed about ten years ago by a coalition of business interests and professional organizations called the Partnership for 21st Century Skills (www.p21.org/). Its focus on a framework of needed complex skills has coalesced into a movement that a number of professional organizations and government entities have endorsed or joined. The position of this coalition—especially of members Partnership for 21st Century Skills (P21), the State Educational Technology Directors Association (SETDA), and the International Society for Technology in Education (ISTE)—is well presented in its call-to-action report *Maximizing the Impact: The Pivotal Role of Technology in a 21st Century Education System* (2007). The members of the coalition are concerned that American education needs substantial reform in objectives and processes. They are propelled by three considerations:

1. The United States is losing its position as the world leader in education, a loss that will inevitably result in economic and cultural declines in comparison with other developed nations. The blame for the current shakiness in our relative economic position is laid at the door of the schoolhouse and is not to be confused with the recession of 2007 and beyond that was precipitated by the financial sector. Many politicians and pundits have challenged the adequacy of American education by using international comparisons to buttress their argument. Some of the spokespersons for this position argue that the United States should adopt the curriculums of higher-achieving countries. (We have serious objections to this proposal. Actually, our usual curriculums are very similar to those in countries where average test scores are higher.) Moreover, many advocates argue that we should have national curriculum standards and measures in the belief that many schools and districts have wandered from the best path. (This is already being actualized, with most states having adopted the Common Core State Standards as their curriculum for English language arts/literacy and mathematics.)

Whether or not we agree with the proposals to standardize curricula, the Partnership and its coalition members are very concerned about indications that we are falling behind other countries and need to take strong steps to reverse the downward trend. Of course, other groups and individuals have been studying educational systems in the United States and beyond, comparing their effects on student achievement, and making recommendations to reform our education system (Common Core, 2009; McKinsey, 2007; Mourshed, Chijioke, & Barber, 2010; OECD, in press; Tucker, 2011; Wagner, 2008). The very title of Wagner's book, *The Global Achievement Gap: Why Even Our Best Schools Don't Teach the New Survival Skills Our Children Need—and What We Can Do About It*, conveys fervently the need to move beyond the status quo in most schools and the consequences to the lives of young people and to the U.S. economy if we do not.

2. Many of our schools have been slow to incorporate developments in technology, particularly multimedia, communications, information access, and integrated use of the Web 2.0 tools, despite the considerable benefits to be realized by doing so. The authors of *Maximizing the Impact* call for a near-term implementation of ICT into schooling—that ICT not be left to gradual adoption led slowly and unevenly by the more energetic teachers and schools. As we write, there is considerable activity in this direction, but certainly only a beginning has been made in most schools and districts compared with the possibilities. The federal position is likely to have a considerable effect because the federal government can inject monetary incentives to accelerate progress.

3. Current preservice education and professional development are not supplying teachers with the knowledge and skills needed to provide the education currently demanded. Essentially, the coalition argues that to incorporate ICT involves almost as much new learning by faculties as by students. The heart of this argument is that our teachers are seriously behind the times and that the problem lies with teacher education programs.

The Partnership movement has a good head of steam. Several national organizations, such as the Association for Supervision and Curriculum Development (ASCD), have adopted the position of the Partnership as their focus for the next several years. Recent international comparisons of achievement, such as those by the Organisation for Economic Co-operation and Development (OECD, 2011), have alarmed much of the public. Within-nation data, such as on dropout rates in high school and male enrollment in higher education, have caused widespread concern, particularly in light of highly publicized and well-funded initiatives by the federal government. That the movement will have a long half-life appears certain at this time. A considerable literature is being generated, and spokespersons are appearing at national and regional educational conferences.

THE SKILLS IN BRIEF

The literature is built around the following knowledge, skills, and expertise that the Partnership/ISTE/SETDA believe are keys to a productive life in the globalized and digitized 21st century:

- **Core subjects**—English, reading, or language arts; world languages; arts; mathematics; economics; science; geography; history; government and civics
- **21st-century themes**—global awareness; financial, economic, business, and entrepreneurial literacy; civic literacy; health literacy
- **Learning and innovation skills**—creativity and innovation skills; critical thinking and problem solving skills; communication and collaboration skills
- **Information, media, and technology skills**—information literacy; media literacy; ICT literacy
- **Life and career skills**—flexibility and adaptability; initiative and self-direction; social and cross-cultural skills; productivity and accountability; leadership and responsibility (P21, SETDA, & ISTE, 2007, p. 5)

As is typical with many of us in education, we do not want to omit good content from our recommendations; thus, the list above leaves us with a need to prioritize and focus. The terms used to describe the 21st-century skills are not standardized throughout the literature, but most authors and publications about 21st-century skills emphasize the following ones. *Importantly,* educators must master their own set of teaching skills (or models) to teach students these crucial 21st-century skills. What we've tried to do is study the recommendations from many sources, combine them with our experience and knowledge of the field, and address those that are most critical for advancing student learning and immediately expanding learning opportunities in our schools.

ICT Literacy

Information and communications technology (ICT) literacy is on everyone's 21st-century-skills list. But the emphasis is not just on use of hardware. The vital skills are cognitive: learning to inquire, to build and test ideas, to categorize, to summarize, to make decisions based on information and experience, and to act on these decisions while continuously collecting new information. These essential cognitive skills have been with us a long time, and they continue to be essential as the opportunities to use them expand beyond our immediate setting. We discuss these skills in greater detail later in this chapter. However, recall (from Chapter Three) that everybody on the emerging platform must also learn to use the new devices and their applications. The caveat: A student can have a lovely bunch of ICT skills but still be unable to inquire effectively or integrate the information garnered from an inquiry.

We believe that the technical and cognitive skills that make a person ICT literate are best taught in the processes of the core curriculum where they are put to work immediately rather than in separate "computer literacy" classes where the new skills are applied later. The basic inductive models of teaching, including scientific inquiry models, can be applied to implement these skills.

Deshler, Palincsar, Biancarosa, and Nair (2007) speak directly to the complex problem of helping students learn not only how to access ICT applications but how to inquire (see, particularly, pp. 45–46). Their entire book emphasizes the need for better ways of helping struggling adolescent readers. But, when they discuss ICT literacy, they point out that students who are decent readers and "may be facile at locating and activating tools" (p. 46) often need explicit instruction on inquiry processes, that is, on building questions to guide inquiry and developing the inductive tools for collecting and organizing data relevant to their questions. In a real sense, the ability to use ICT productively includes learning to read and write in the conventional sense, learning to use the digital tools, and learning to conduct inquiries.

Despite the criticisms many digital advocates make of teachers, most teachers have basic ICT skills, but unfortunately they have not been directed toward teaching/learning as much as they need to be. Many need more advanced skills, but they have much to build on. We emphasize that the major need is for the process of building hybrid courses that have students and teachers using ICT rather than seeing ICT skills as skills to be learned and then transmitted, *en bloc*, to the students.

Digital Tools

Here we will look only at immediate needs. New tools may appear to replace the ones in greatest use today, but many parents and students possess the tools to take advantage of distance opportunities today. Where they do not, teachers can remedy the problem. Currently needed tools are these:

- Word processing, presentation, and production software
- Graphics, surveys, and modeling tools
- Digital-picture and video-editing software (and photo sharing)
- Basic Internet resources accessed via search engines/browsers (databases, libraries)
- Communication and collaboration systems (e.g., wikis, blogs, VoIP such as Skype, email, texting, podcasts)
- Spreadsheet programs such as Excel

In addition, mastery of interactive whiteboard technology is increasingly useful. At first we underestimated the impact of touch-screen technology, but we now think that it is very important.

However well the classroom is equipped, equipping all students is vital. The Maine Learning Technology Initiative has led the way, and we hope that in these tough economic times it will be able to continue until every student in the state is equipped and connected. Essentially, *all* students need to be equipped with laptops and basic programs and with smartphone technologies as well. We say "laptop" with a caveat: By the time this book is printed, some visionary may have produced a device that will replace the laptop as the educational device of choice.

We have much to learn and many skills to develop. We can manage all this. The leading edge of technology will continue to feed us useful procedures and devices, and we will learn them and increase our capability. And, just as technology has become easier to use and more accessible over the last two decades, we have confidence that technology providers will continue to make their products even easier to use. For example, instead of the expensive office suites that that many of us have purchased, students can go to Google Docs (http://docs.google.com/) and use very similar software free to create word-processing documents, presentations, and spreadsheets.

Basic ICT skills need to become pervasive in education. However, teachers need not be intimidated by strident rhetoric—they have learned and can learn what is needed to create the new platforms for learning. On the other hand, in some quarters there seems to be a belief that the digital skills will appear naturally as computer and smartphone experience grows. That is not necessarily true. Agee and Altarriba's (2009) study indicates that the use of specific applications does not necessarily lead to general ICT competence—or interest. And basic, traditional literacy competencies—reading and writing—are critical. Poor readers and writers will be ICT handicapped.

Cultural Literacy and Global Awareness

One of the most striking characteristics of the ICT explosion and the rise of a global economy is their effect on relations near and far. The nature of our culture is changing, generating a considerable need for intracultural understanding. The peoples of the world are sharing words and images, and intercultural interactions are becoming common-place as a global culture emerges. The implications are apparent as nations have become interdepen-dent, economies are becoming unified, and we as individuals are in con-tact with, well, almost everyone. A provincial perspective today can have devastating consequences.

> **Why Should We Expect That Integrating ICT Into Curricula and Courses Will Improve Learning?**
>
> We all need to ask ourselves whether bringing ICT more forcefully into education will result in one or more kinds of improvements in student learning.
>
> ICT is not an area where we can rely on a history of studies that lead to the "what works" type of endorsement. However, there is an enormous knowledge base on existing approaches to teaching the prominent skills—information from previous generations of the applications of media to curriculum and instruction. Although the digital media are dramatic, the use of media in education has a long and instructive history. In Chapter Twelve we will review selected relevant research, including open inquiries into the evidence rather than just the rhetoric of settled conclusions.

Our new school needs to emphasize global perspectives. Learning how to inquire across cultural boundaries is incredibly important. Fortunately, the models of teaching and learning that can accomplish this level of education already exist. ICT enhances them. We ourselves sometimes forget how much we have been changed by the digital revolution. In the last month, we have been in contact with people from six countries without giving that fact much attention. Our travel agent of ten years lives in another country, and today we sent a set of DVD demonstrations of teaching models to Australia. During the last few weeks, our children have visited three other countries.

We desperately need hybrid courses in the global social studies as well as increased emphasis on global literacy in the other subject areas. Fortunately, we have good designs and plenty of materials. We need to just do it, to para-phrase NIKE. (See the journals *Social Education* and *Social Studies for the Young Learner;* the *Teacher's Discovery* website at www.teachersdiscovery.com/; and

Bennett & Berson, 2007, which contains a large number of technology-based lesson plans for social studies, K–12.)

Collaborative and Cooperative Skills

We need each other. We always have, but the price of failure to work with others near and far has become unsustainable. Schools need to develop a rich culture to teach students to work and play together. In fact, the campus will be a very important place in the future because it is the major social laboratory for the young. As they reach out into cyberspace and information and ideas zip back from global sites, they need each other for perspective. The simpler cooperative learning models must pervade the school, and the most complex models—cooperative/inquiry models, group investigation, and jurisprudential inquiry—should propel major inquiries. This is another area where professional development can draw on considerable numbers of teachers and other personnel who have wide experience with cooperative models of teaching. From the simpler, direct, cooperative strategies (Slavin, 1983, 1994) to the more complex, human relations–building models (Johnson & Johnson, 1999) and the procedures for organizing students for inquiry (Sharan & Shachar, 1988), the vision of cooperation can be enhanced. Social media have limitless possibilities.

The large and positive research on and experience with cooperative learning should be put to work here. Students can be organized into small—two- to three-person—groups both to study computer applications and carry out inquiries in substantive areas. Generally, cooperative learning has both academic and social benefits for most students of all ages. However, most can also profit from instruction on how to work together productively. Some simple guidelines include the following:

- Keep groups small. You can begin with groups of two when students are unaccustomed to cooperative work.
- Rotate group membership. A cooperative group is not a marriage!
- Have all students take turns as "recorders." Avoid assigning one as the primary recorder or chairperson.
- Ensure that all students are responsible for all aspects of an inquiry. Division of labor is less productive than inquiry by all with results shared among members.
- Remember that diversity is an asset in cooperative learning. Students with differing learning histories benefit from working with each other, and often feelings of camraderie develop among students of both similar and different backgrounds.

A myth that the best students are not well suited to cooperative activities is just that—a myth. Actually, students who do well working alone tend to do well in cooperative situations. Training on working cooperatively tends to benefit everybody. Listening to and understanding the perspectives of others is the foundation of building strong learning communities (see IASCE, 2011).

The school as an academic and social base has never been more important. This platform harbors our young people and gives them the sense of community that is so vital to a strong concept of self.

Personal and Social Responsibility

The formative assessment of academic and social learning is owned by students as well as staff. Clarity of achievement enables students to see what they are learning and where they need to work harder or more skillfully. They set goals and become students of their own learning; metacognition (learning to think about how to learn) becomes a normal part of study. While tending to themselves, the students also engage in projects for social benefit. The school is decorated with their efforts to make it attractive and comfortable. They look for opportunities to contribute to the lives of people who may be far removed geographically but be close to them in cyberspace. It is interesting to imagine a platform where a certain amount of education takes place in campus courses and a certain amount is independent study through online offerings. In other words, students can be taught, early, that part of their education is through self-study with distance support.

Collaboration can be near and far, as emphasized by the connected teaching movement. But near is critical, and the skills learned right where we live are the ones that make distance collaboration live.

To teach democratic collaboration and inquiry, the school needs to be a democratic, collaborative community (that is, faculty, administration, students, and all Responsible Parties comprise the community). That community needs to dig into problems and create solutions. By working together, problems of attendance (through team spirit), civility (through eradicating divisive and bullying behaviors), and energy for learning (through collaborative inquiry) will be solved. In this community, the students learn social behavior that will increase the quality of their entire lives. They have unity without stifling conformity.

Creativity and Innovation

Convergent thinking enables students to focus on and drive for mastery of knowledge and skills from outside. Divergent thinking plays with information, concepts, pictures, sounds, and objects. Things are moved around, and surprises appear. The process is what the great Bill Gordon called *serious playfulness,* an oxymoron that captures the essence of metaphoric thinking. Ideas that were born on different cognitive planets are placed next to each other, on top of each other, inside each other. Environments populated with analogies lure students into a divergent state. It is these environments that permit our minds to innovate.

The Partnership emphasizes creativity in a competitive world context—as a survival skill that gives people and organizations a competitive edge. That may be, but we see it as giving people quality of life as well. Playing and inventing gives us a better life, a more humorous and adaptable workplace, and new understandings that make the familiar, as Gordon expressed it, strange—giving new life to the prosaic. Some very well developed approaches to teaching are available in this area (see Joyce et al., 2009).

> *Authors' note:* Rather than teaching our young to compete on global terms, we might achieve more by helping them learn to enrich their own social and economic contexts. You don't win by marketing a thin culture well. You enhance yourself and others by building a culturally rich society that markets itself. That has been the best part of the American global relationship.

Critical Thinking and Problem Solving

The Partnership literature speaks of critical thinking and problem solving in the same breath as creativity. The essence of these skills is to scrutinize evidence and conclusions carefully and view alternative courses of action with a healthy skepticism, seeking better alternatives. The school and community become laboratories where issues are faced, problems identified, relevant information gathered and sifted, and solutions generated and assessed.

Most problems that merit solving are not produced by crises. They are found in the ordinary course of living and working together. They are not PROBLEMS in the "OMG!" sense. Sharing time, space, and resources requires constant adjustment in school as it does in the community and private and public organizations. Regional, national, and global life requires analogous activity to modulate arrangements. Crisis does happen, and when it does, those best prepared are those who are accustomed to thinking about the conditions of life in their day-to-day social environments and solving the continuous little problems that inhabit the landscape. The basic inductive models of teaching are well tested and provide a strong foundation in this area.

ENHANCING AND FOCUSING THE SKILLS

Inevitably the meaning of the term *skill* has to be unpacked in order to use it as the focus of reform. The dictionary definitions run up scale of complexity, beginning with

"knowledge of the means or methods for accomplishing a task"

and then

"the ability to use one's knowledge effectively in execution or performance"

and then

"a learned power of doing a thing competently"

and, finally,

"developed or acquired aptitude or ability."

These levels all come into play in discussions of 21st-century skills. The first three are important to success, but the fourth captures the intent of the movement. Knowing how to accomplish specific tasks, being able to do so, and possessing "a learned power" all convey the positive results of study. An increase in aptitude—of capacity—is the overarching goal. Learning more, being able to do more, and experiencing success develop the ability to learn.

As we indicated above, the consequence of 21st-century learning is an increase in what has traditionally been referred to as intelligence. The belief in genetic intellectual capacity, which has been promoted by some schools of psychology and the focus of certain practices in testing and test interpretation, has influenced decades of educational practice—to the detriment of too many children. Intellectual capacity can be enhanced considerably through education, ensuring that our children have optimum learning opportunities conducive to the development of cognitions and skills.

HOW TO USE THE SKILLS

As we build new courses and curricula, we can use the formulation of 21st-century skills as a screen, asking which we are incorporating into our plan. Basically, they all suggest teaching students how to learn in ways that increase capacity, that is, intelligent behavior. Capacity is seen as learnable; it embodies an optimistic view of learners and, therefore, of schooling. As we consider assessing learning (see Chapter Eleven) we need to consider how to measure the development of capacity. Students who have inauspicious capacity are not cured simply by learning more information and skills. They succeed by learning how to learn in the course of acquiring information and skills. Tools for self-education should drive the curriculum, including the conceptual schemes (maps) that provide access to knowledge and skill.

Characteristics of Inductive Approaches

Information and communication technologies are providing access to information to an extent that individuals have never had before. Unless teachers and students build the tools to organize and use this information, their minds will be virtually inundated by the sheer mass of material. The unprecedented possibility of elevating education will slip away if it is not accompanied by those tools—and they are inductive in nature.

We will look at the character of inductive teaching, its relationship to other models of teaching, its effects, how it combines with other models, the social contexts in which it is accepted, and the professional development needed to make it work. We need to be clear that the important discussions about inductive teaching and learning are not ideological. A large portion of education discussion is around manufactured dichotomies—such as "Shall we have child-centered or content-centered learning?" Inductive approaches to teaching and learning rise above that type of discussion. Teaching and learning inductively embrace content and the capacity of the learner equally and elevate both. Students need to learn to discover concepts. Teachers can teach them to build ideas and can also provide ideas upon which the students can reflect.

Let's begin by looking at the characteristics of inductive curriculum, teaching, and learning.

Learning to Inquire

The inductive curriculum is built on learning to inquire. The teacher and student become researchers. They create knowledge and are committed to develop their skills to do so.

A researcher, whether a beginner or an advanced scholar, seeks to populate the inquiry with information. The information, once gathered, does not organize itself. The research mind has to organize it into categories so that it has a "location" in the mind and can be moved around—manipulated—in search of greater understanding. Information changes its character when it is organized. Building categories enriches both the information and the mind that harbors it.

Thus, researchers seek information, organize it into sets—lists of similar information units—and then build categories by comparing and contrasting the attributes of the units in the sets. As researchers proceed, they study how to build categories more skillfully and how to build and test ideas so that the bits of information are connected in conceptual systems. Those systems are the key to both the power to understand whatever domain is being investigated and the ability to use the learning purposefully, and they are the key to long-term retention as well. The structures of the advanced disciplines are made up of ways of collecting information, ways of organizing that information into categories, and ways of integrating those categories into conceptual systems.

Borrowing From the Disciplines: An Active Enterprise

The student researcher can borrow categories built by others but also has to make them his own. The highly skilled teacher at every level knows that she can introduce the student to ideas—even to the structures of the disciplines—but also knows that the student has to operate on them, reflect on them, and possess them. Just grinding them into memory makes them shadows on the edge of the mind. And they will slip away. A little after a course on the history of art, how many of us have said to ourselves or others, "I used to think I knew what Impressionism is, but . . . ." If we say something like that, then we know that the category, Impressionism, was not really established in our mind. We had impressions of impressionism but had not built the category by examining examples to the point where we possessed a working concept of it.

Building on a Natural Talent

Creating categories is inborn, but it needs to be nourished to reach its potential. Infants learn not only to discriminate particular words connected to specific objects and actions but also to generalize by placing objects and actions together. Thus they learn foods, tables and chairs, things we can drink, and so on. Quite early they can distinguish houses from cars, underwear from outerwear—heaps of things. They *cannot* resist piling things into categories.

Nourishing the Ability to Build Ideas

There is a long history of research on forms of inductive teaching, including studies built around the processes of the disciplines, those built around the process of categorization as such, and those that are built on cooperative inquiry.

A major set of innovations developed between the late 1950s and the 1980s was built around the academic disciplines. Some, as in biology, remain the orientation of secondary school and college courses. By the mid-1970s Bredderman (1973, 1983) was able to review 57 studies involving 3 strategies for teaching science-based inquiry skills in 900 classrooms with more than 25,000 elementary school children. The conceptual/inquiry curricula generated more learning of content, concepts, methods of inquiry, and attitudes toward science. The findings embraced all disciplines and both integrated and separate-subject approaches. They applied to children of all grades, all SES levels, English-language learners, and students qualified for special education (at mild to moderate levels).

Almy (1970) demonstrated not only that combining inductive courses across the curriculum in the second grade succeeded in teaching scientific inquiry to young children but that doing so increased their power to think logically.

This type of work continues to the present. The following indicate the ongoing confirmation of the strength of the inductive methods in studies of different types.

Baumert, J., Kunter, M., Blum, W., Brunner, M., Voss, T., Jordan, W., Klussman, U., Krauss, S., Neubrand, M., & Tsai, Y.-N. (2010). Teachers' mathematical knowledge, cognitive activation in the classroom, and student progress. *American Educational Research Journal, 47*, 133–180. Connects teachers' mathematical knowledge and engagement in inquiry to student learning.

(Continued)

(Continued)

Essentially, demonstrating mathematical thinking processes to students has a positive effect.

Burkam, D. T., Lee, V. E., & Smerdon, B. A. (1997). Gender and science learning early in high school: Subject matter and laboratory experiences. *American Educational Research Journal, 34*, 297–331. Reports a large-scale study of tenth-grade achievement in science with a particularly interesting conclusion: that hands-on laboratory experiences, while benefitting all students, are of particular benefit to females.

Klauer, K., & Phye, G. (2008). Inductive reasoning: A training approach. *Review of Educational Research, 78*, 85–123. Focuses on the effect of curricula designed to teach students inductive processes. Looking at the results of 74 studies involving 3,600 children, the authors found positive effects on measures of cognitive functioning—essentially, general intelligence—as well as positive effects on academic performance.

We believe that this history conveys a strong message to designers of both hybrid campus courses and distance courses. Essentially, learning how to learn inductively can be taught and pays off when it is used.

AN ETHICAL ASPECT

People do not live in a medium of information and skill alone—an ethical dimension must be central in the education of our children. *Empathy* is a vital part of productive and satisfying relationships, whether at close quarters with family, friends, and neighbors or in more physically distant interactions in communities, in nations, and across the planet. Learning to put oneself in the place of the other is the core of a working morality. The moral dimension of education needs to be amplified considerably. Ethical and moral considerations need to be woven through all aspects of personal and organizational life.

HOW NEW AND UNUSUAL ARE THE "SKILLS"?

As the skills are presented by the Partnership, we see them in three categories: content to be taught, instructional processes, and digital skills. Let's look at each in turn.

Curricular content—The content is familiar. Little in the literature proposes content that is not in most curriculum guides in one form or another. We all know that we have uneven implementation of key curricula and need to do better. But there is nothing an educator would not recognize easily. In fact, much of what the Partnership recommends has been in curriculum guides for years. Noneducators can easily believe that changing terms, as from *objectives and evaluation* to *standards and benchmarks*, will make a difference. The difference in the terms is inconsequential, however. Whether we will support teachers with adequate professional learning opportunities—that is significant.

Methods of teaching—Here again, the ways of teaching described in the Partnership literature can be enhanced considerably by using strategies like inductive teaching that are within reach of educators. The education literature contains a large storehouse of models of teaching that can serve as a foundation. Many teachers need larger repertoires than they currently employ, and the real issue is whether appropriate learning opportunities will be made available to them.

A CLUSTER OF ADVOCATES

The Partnership has performed an important service by focusing the work of incorporating ICT effectively in education—the 21st-century skills concept is providing a structure that should support the kinds of professional development that will fulfill the digital promises.

Other groups are engaging in parallel and important work. The Council of Chief State School Officers is revisiting the question of what competencies teachers need (CCSSO, 2011), and its conclusions are compatible with the definitions of skills presented in this chapter.

Today's learners need both the academic and global skills and knowledge necessary to navigate the world—attributes and dispositions such as problem solving, curiosity, creativity, innovation, communication, interpersonal skills, the ability to synthesize across disciplines, global awareness, ethics and technological expertise. . . .

Additionally, the core teaching standards stress that teachers build literacy and thinking skills across the curriculum, as well as help learners address multiple perspectives in exploring ideas and solving problems. (CCSSO, 2011, p. 4)

The Singularity Movement

Ray Kurzweil and Peter Diamandis founded Singularity University to provide corporate executives, government agencies, and scholars with seminars and courses to help them think about their immediate needs as they seek to catch up with the futures that are already here. Singularity University promotes the view that technology not only embodies human intelligence but can enhance it and go beyond it to attack enormous problems; in other words, it can comprise an intelligence far beyond our current capability. In a few decades,

> life will take on an altered form that we cannot predict or comprehend in our limited state. . . . Humans and machines so effortlessly and elegantly merge that poor health, the ravages of old age, and even death itself will be things of the past. (Vance, 2010)

This incredible optimism reflects the experience of many of the founders and supporters of Singularity that technology has enabled them to think better and accomplish more—far more—than they could have without it.

Google's cofounder, Larry Page, helped focus the university's mission: "to assemble, educate, and inspire leaders who understand and develop exponentially advancing technologies to address humanity's Grand Challenges" (http://singularityu.org/about/overview/).

Interestingly, a number of federal agencies are grappling with the problems of incorporating ICT into education. The Federal Communications Commission is looking into the possibilities of using broadband connections to improve education and, simultaneously, to generate greater equity by ensuring that all households (and schools) are appropriately connected (see Federal Communications Commission, n.d.).

FROM VISION TO ACTION

Part II concentrates on the development of curriculums, courses, and schools that reflect the visions in Chapters One through Six. What does the vision look like when turned into action? The school becomes a center of inquiry for teachers and students—thus professional learning and student learning are parts of the same culture. As we move into the practical realms of development, we need to take a moment to ask, How different are the new skills from those the profession has known and used during the last half of the 20th century?

SUMMARIES IN THE WORDS OF TEACHERS AND STUDENTS

We keep running into teachers and students who add bits to our notebook.

I have been very pleased with the things we have learned to do with the Smartboard. But the most surprising is how easily I am able to model writing. Moving sentences around, changing words, trying on titles—this is a natural hybrid that really makes instruction more effective.

. . . Our Collegial Teacher

Every month we email our newspaper and put it on our webpage. The first page usually gives the results of one of our studies. With parents, grandparents, other relatives, and other community members, we have a distribution of about 300. Our report on conditions in Haiti received many replies, and our summary of information from the census surprised us and many of our contacts. Sharing writing on our blog is almost magical. And we can share stuff that's not just part of assignments— we can share text, photos, videos that are related to things we've already studied.

. . . Our Industrious Student

We have an information feast. But—learning to organize our minds, always essential, is now a critical necessity. Otherwise we will find ourselves under a virtual pile of odds and ends and the sheer mass will trivialize everything. The libraries of available material are rich. And you can't just walk around the print library and peek into them. Building concepts has always been the hallmark of intelligent behavior. We ordinary folks may have to increase our capability or lie supine under several million pixels.

. . . Our Reflective Observer

Make no mistake—we all have to become more proficient with digital tools or we are at their mercy. The tools themselves are amoral. If we thought that poor textbooks were a rotten shame, and we have been living with lots of them, these new gadgets can deliver bad information badly at a rate that textbook writers never dreamed of.

. . . Our Worried Techie

Learning complex skills requires introducing and explaining their rationale, demonstrating them, and helping the students practice them until they can be used easily with new content and problems. The skills need to become available at the level of "second nature."

. . . Our Reflective Teacher

Part II

Important Things to Just Do Right Now

Students, teachers, parents, and community are part of the major makeover of education that is in its early stages. While technology has had a significant impact on homes and in some schools, we've barely begun to reap its benefits for the total education of our students. On the home platform, although there are terrible inequities, Internet access, distance/online courses, social networks, texting, Skyping, and exchanges of pictures and other material are now present in a good number of settings. However, level of access declines as socioeconomic status declines: students in less affluent homes have less media and less access to the digital libraries and Web 2.0 tools. Parallel development is happening in schools, but again there are inequities, again related to socioeconomic status (SES). We have glimpses of the possibilities.

We are also mindful that the spread of technology will not, by itself, bring about needed changes in schooling. The potential of the promises for curriculum and instruction will be won by deliberate decision making and hard work. Teams of educators, with technical support, will have to redevelop courses. In the long run, new modes of student interaction with curriculum may emerge. In the short run, most progress will be forged by making ICT the servant of the well-known curriculum areas. Some striking variations and additions will appear, but for now, let's make progress by building on the best of the familiar.

We need to organize the Responsible Parties in each school and begin the disciplined process of taking advantage of opportunities. We need also to make some long overdue changes in how education is conducted—changes needed before *Silicon Valley* entered the vocabulary and before the Apple had been held out to us. Here are six of them, the ones around which the rest of this book is built.

1. **Develop and adapt hybrid courses.** In these, technology enhances campus courses. It is deliberately incorporated (blended) into the core curriculum areas, K–12. At the same time, we need to create the professional development that will prepare school faculties to blend campus-based approaches and ICT into the hybrid courses and adapt such courses developed elsewhere.

2. **Begin rethinking the secondary education platform.** Develop policies for distance credit, build hybrids, and redo the daily and annual schedules.

3. **Provide equipment and ensure access to basic software.** The appropriate ICT devices and applications—and the technical support needed to use them—must be available to *everyone concerned*. That means ensuring that our 50 million students, their homes, and their 120,000 schools are well equipped. Our entire country needs to become a hotspot.

4. **Aggressively address the upgrading of the literacy curriculum in all subjects, K–12.** Literacy must be addressed in all subject areas. Help for struggling readers must be available in all grades and all subjects.

5. **Reinvent assessment.** Implement performance-oriented, formative assessment so that information about progress and needs is embedded in instruction and flows smoothly to the people who can use it: teachers, students, parents and caregivers, and support staff.

6. **Broaden and deepen the governance structure of schools.** Leadership through collaboration must be established as the normal way of doing business.

Let's look at each of these as gateways to immediate progress and as laying the groundwork for a promising future.

1. DEVELOP AND ADAPT HYBRID COURSES

All six avenues listed above are important, but the fulfillment of the promises will be severely limited unless the campus and our digital universe become closely connected. Building the connection starts with the development of the hybrid course—the campus course that scoops up the resources available in the New Library, including digital resources available on DVD and the distance offerings. *This work can begin immediately to the benefit of both educator and student learning.*

At both the elementary and secondary levels, teachers study as individuals and as members of professional learning communities. At times, they work together to determine where ICT applications can best support student learning. In this way, they can support each other in developing technological expertise. They can determine, through their study of student responses to lessons and learning experiences, how to refine and expand the curriculum provided for and with their students. Curriculum development that shapes what happens in elementary classrooms and secondary courses becomes part of professional development—where it belongs.

The faculties in schools can develop hybrids in the core curriculum areas, course by course. And they can adapt courses built elsewhere. Hopefully states will invest in searching out developments in hybrid courses and in their own development of hybrids and make these available to school faculties. States and districts also need to invest in developing the technical assistance that faculties will need. Professional development can concentrate on supporting in-school teacher activity, including whatever technical support teachers may need. As state-funded development of curriculum frameworks produces prototype courses, these can be made available to faculties everywhere for possible adaptation to their circumstances and particular purposes.

2. BEGIN RETHINKING THE SECONDARY EDUCATION PLATFORM

Several problems that beset secondary education need to be dealt with simultaneously. One is driven by the availability of distance courses. Sociocultural change is impacting the conduct of education. Independent distance study is exerting tremendous influence, requiring a redesign of schools as platforms, including the nature of their partnership with home and student.

Coughlin (2010) elegantly summarizes the dilemma of today's high school (his comments apply equally to K–8):

> They may choose a path that would define them in the future as mere certification mills, verifying student learning that has taken place. Or they may redefine themselves as collaborative, relevant environments in which students build the expanded skill sets they need. . . . It is not yet clear which path schools will choose. (p. 48)

Coughlin coins the term *information emancipation* to connote what is happening as both inquiry and formal course taking have become available. Home and student are not bound to the print library or instruction in the school. Not only can the imagination roam freely through the cyberworld, but virtually every course in the curriculum is now available at distance *and* many providers are accredited to provide K–12 instruction. The student can present completed courses to the school to fulfill requirements for diplomas. However, where schools have fewer offerings than are desirable, distance courses can be a godsend, as in the case of our Charley.

However, several problems were apparent before distance courses became an option.

The "empty senior year phenomenon" occurred as school schedules used shorter and shorter daily segments or periods and more and more students were completing graduation requirements or nearly completing them before the senior year.

In addition, a large number of students were not completing graduation requirements at all! Nearly 30 percent nationally do not graduate, and the percentage is much higher in some schools, districts, and even whole states.

Much of the reason for poor academic performance is simply inadequate reading and writing skills.

We know that smaller high schools are good both socially and academically (see Leithwood & Janttzi, 2009). Many of our high schools are simply too large. This can be ameliorated in a number of ways: making small ones out of big ones is a fairly obvious solution.

We grapple with these problem and related needs in Chapter Nine. Although distance courses and cyberschools may change how solutions emerge, in nearly all cases, local high schools need to assess their situations and work to improve themselves. Some are already making good progress, but many need very badly to institute redesign efforts.

3. PROVIDE EQUIPMENT AND ENSURE ACCESS TO BASIC SOFTWARE

Equity in education cannot be achieved without provision of needed devices and software to *all* students. For those who object because of cost, we ask you to look at expenditures that have little or no positive effect on students (e.g., workbooks, routine adoption of textbooks in content areas where there has been little change, class sets of novels, testing that does not provide information that directly informs instruction). Perhaps even examine the research on class size and see that expenditures to reduce pupil-teacher ratios may have little effect on outcomes. Current per-pupil expenditures run about $10,000 per year on average in the United States. For about 5 percent of that, or about $500 per year, ICT needs can be met within a single year. Subsequent annual costs would be substantially lower. The investment *will* pay off. Truly this is an investment rather than an expense.

4. AGGRESSIVELY ADDRESS THE UPGRADING OF THE LITERACY CURRICULUM IN ALL SUBJECTS, K–12

For decades, 30 percent of our nation's students have left the primary grades unable to read and write adequately. Make no mistake: Suburban schools are not immune—15 to 20 percent is about the right figure there. And the ongoing disaster taking place in the lowest SES schools is well known—as many as 60 percent of students in these schools enter high school without basic literacy skills. The other disaster area is male students; the average male is at about the 30th percentile of female achievement in reading and writing. Almost three-fifths of college students are females. Only 35–40 percent of enrolled first-year males graduate from college in four years, while two-thirds of females do. (Just imagine the difference in cost!) Literacy is basic to solving SES- and gender-based disproportionalities. Much is known about supporting students' literacy development, but application of this knowledge (implementation) has been slow.

5. REINVENT ASSESSMENT

The U.S. Department of Education is soliciting bids on contracts to build new tests that, hopefully, will bear a close relationship to curriculum, emphasize what students know and can do, focus on gains, and provide diagnostic information and evidence about how much students are learning. In other words, federal policy (and states and districts will follow this lead) may be leading us toward a much more meaningful and understandable approach to assessment than the current comparison-oriented tests have been or could be. Development will take time—the question is, how can we improve assessment *now*? Probably the most productive avenue is teacher-developed formative assessment within the context of the curriculum being taught. We believe this is feasible, can be implemented by teams within schools, and will provide information that helps teachers design instruction and students monitor their progress. As new formal tests are built, they can be used alongside the instruments generated by practitioners.

6. BROADEN AND DEEPEN THE GOVERNANCE STRUCTURE OF SCHOOLS

The federal government can and should develop initiatives, states can and should adopt standards and benchmarks, districts can and should set goals and provide consultant support—but the educational environment is in the school and home. The field of educational leadership has concentrated on the principal and, less frequently, on teacher leaders. Only a few scholars have emphasized the development of a shared democratic leadership in the principal/staff complex (Blase & Blase, 2000; Glickman, 1998). But it is necessary here. The digital revolution cannot be done by fiat, and bottom-up initiatives must be broadly supported in order to work.

We must create a broad and deep governance system today. Home and school have to form a richly connected partnership. Administrators, faculty, and parents need to be active participants. And the community needs to be involved as well. Governance builds the climate of the adult community, and that climate determines how well the education of children will be conducted and how the school will become ever better.

STEPS

In Chapters Seven through Ten, we will discuss and illustrate steps to be taken to fulfill the promises.

Chapter Seven: We begin at the school level with the formation of a democratic decision-making process. Why begin at the school level? Because whether initiatives are made at the school level or other levels of the system—district, state, or federal—education happens at the school level and the condition of the school's governance will be a major factor. Governance at this level determines whether the school can improve itself or adapt initiatives made at the other levels. A number of teachers and administrators we have talked to do not realize that inductive inquiry—individual or cooperative—is more powerful than drill-and-practice teaching and provides learning that endures (and generally better test results on performance measures). Cooperative governance that leads to the study of teaching will help correct such misimpressions and legitimize the teaching of intelligent inquiry as a major goal of the school.

Chapter Eight: Developing and adapting hybrid courses will be the most important factor in effectively integrating ICT into formal education.

Learning how to develop hybrids is currently one of the most important needs in the professional development arena.

Chapter Nine: High schools vitally need a new style of platform and much more collaboration with the home platform. The high school as we have known it is about to change. The major question is whether the current institution takes a proactive approach or is merely acted upon.

Chapter Ten: The term *development* in staff and professional development has always been somewhat ambiguous. In the next few years, teachers will need to develop and adapt hybrid courses, making the process of development central. It will help deal with the issue mentioned above, that some educators believe retro forms of drill and practice or retention of students in grade level are the way to success.

7 The Responsible Parties

*The Essential Local
Democratic Process*

We should prize involvement. We want to include those who will work to build the best possible education for the children in their community. Interested parties should not be excluded, even if it is not obvious that they have an institutional right to participation. That said, most members will be from the local constituencies of the school, the people and organizations who serve and are served directly by the school.

. . . Our Reflective Observer

COMMENTS FROM RESPONSIBLE PARTY
MEMBERS OF AN ELEMENTARY SCHOOL

We were just about to adopt a supplementary online program on phonics for our fifth and sixth graders who are struggling readers when our Literacy Team discovered research indicating that only a few students at that level have problems with basic phonics. In other words, the students might have been studying what they already knew. The English teachers used the Names Test (Cunningham, 1990, 2005) to study a sample of those students and, sure enough, found that for most of these struggling readers, their phonics were in fine shape. We would have wasted a lot of student time and money!

We realized that we were thinking in terms of a cultural stereotype—that poor readers always have phonics problems. That legend was promoted by the people who were trying to sell us their program. This is not the only time that having our Responsible Parties organization has led us to meaningful research.

... Fifth-Grade Parent Representative

Is technology dangerous? My goodness! When we (our Responsible Parties) decided to make the neighborhood a hot spot, the laptops started travelling between school and home. Also, more kids began to lobby for digital devices at home—computers, tablets, etc. Some of our parents began to learn what is out there on the web and didn't like everything they saw. They raised objections to the principal and addressed the school board.

Fortunately, our Responsible Parties had made the decision and included a vote by the faculty and the parent representative council. So we announced an open meeting on the subject where the advantages and disadvantages of creating the hot spot were discussed. We also found some reports by other schools that had made the same decision and had experience with whether students explored the sites our complaining group were afraid they would. Also, we found a consultant who was very forceful in saying that parents who actively talked with their children and set clear limits about what would not be accessed had few problems.

We have made it easy for any parent whose child took his or her investigation into suspicious territory to contact the technology committee and ask for help. Actually, just knowing they were not alone was the most important thing in defusing what might have been an unpleasant series of confrontations.

... Fifth-Grade Team Leader

When someone suggested that we move the neighborhood public library branch into the school and keep it open all evening, I thought they were nuts. I couldn't imagine the city and the city library services and the board of education doing anything cooperatively. Clearly it would save money and build the book and magazine collection dramatically. And we had several other evening functions that would fit in and could split some of the costs.

Our Responsible Parties liked the idea. They used SurveyMonkey—an online survey tool the district often uses to gather information about curriculum and professional development needs—to gather information from colleagues districtwide. They sent principals and Responsible Party chairs in the other schools the results and rationale for the idea. One of our fourth-grade teachers worked with her students and polled the community (http://polls.zoho.com/) to find out their response to the idea and build awareness. With information from these sources and their belief in the value of expanding access, the Responsible Parties convened meeting after meeting until the city supervisors and downtown library administrators began to give up their objections.

It happened, and it has worked. There have been minor glitches, but it's been a treat to watch kids and parents, sometimes grandparents, exploring and learning together.

... Our Super Librarian

D o we need a broad-based democratic governance process at the school level? We certainly do, for three prominent reasons:

1. Increasing inquiry into available research and options by a community of teachers, parents, administrators, and local institutions

2. Ensuring broad-based decision making on school improvement issues

3. Ensuring support when initiatives get into murky water where what direction to take is unclear

Local school governance influences both the quality of the educational environment and its ability to improve itself. Organizational climate is a profoundly important factor in the success of a change effort at the school, district, state, and national levels. The long history of school improvement initiatives has a simple message: if the social climate of the school is not conducive to change, even promising changes do not last. And school climate depends on school governance. Our ability to deliver on the 21st-century promise will require a broad governance structure in which all stakeholders strive to create the best education possible in their venues.

In most schools, we need to widen participation in the formal governance arrangements and simultaneously build a more complex and dynamic partnership between school and home. In this chapter, we will discuss membership in the group we have for many years called "the Responsible Parties." In Chapter Eleven, we will illustrate the process of broadened governance in a scenario of a school in action.

MEMBERSHIP: PARTNERS IN MORAL PURPOSE

Imagine a two-tiered organization: an assembly having a good-sized membership and a steering committee of, perhaps, a dozen persons.

Certainly the general membership of the Responsible Parties and any smaller leadership group (assembly or steering committee) needs represent a broad base of school and community members who influence what happens in schools. Some of these are obvious.

District Institutional Leaders

The steering committee should include district office personnel responsible for direct support to the school. Large districts often house support personnel in administrative areas. In some states, intermediate support agencies are responsible for providing service to the schools. Representatives of the curriculum, professional development, and special needs departments are important, as are persons representing specific governmental initiatives. In recent years, coordinators of Title I programs, No Child Left Behind, and Reading First have been needed because those programs provide many resources and, frequently, require documented compliance with many regulations of procedures and assessment. However, the reason for including district coordinators is not so they can monitor present rules and regulations. It is their competence and perspective that makes them valuable members of the Responsible Parties. Personnel in these positions frequently have a comparative perspective that can help communities gain understanding about differences in schools, and many are knowledgeable about curriculum and instruction. Importantly, they liaise with the district administration when proposed changes involve budget and procedures.

School Institutional Leaders

Principals and other officials of the school are essential. The principal is responsible for assembling the Responsible Parties and serves as pro tem chairperson as the assembly is brought together and organized and then as ex officio cochairperson. Importantly, while principals should be able to place items on the agenda, they should not control the agenda by themselves and simply look for approval of their ideas. In other words, the principal leads and pilots the process of governance development but in the spirit of developing a democratic organization of Responsible Parties.

Faculty

At small schools, the assembly should include the entire faculty; the steering committee should include representatives elected by the staff. Large staffs need to elect assembly members and steering committee members. Even in large schools, however, when the state of curriculum and instruction is on the table, the entire faculty needs to become involved. In the case of initiatives that affect a few staff members, they need to be fully engaged and keep the rest of the staff informed. When a broad initiative is considered, one that involves several curriculum areas, then the entire faculty needs to be brought into the discussion.

Parents

Parents are vital to student achievement and school renewal efforts. School and home are the gateways to a good education. A larger share of educational experience takes place in homes than in schools. In the 21st century, the partnership between home and school will become more complex and integrated. Increasingly the school will serve the parents as well as the children.

Regular communication between the school and the parents will increase where the school program and school events are the subject as well as communication between staff and parents with respect to particular children. As we have said many times, the school needs to ensure that every student has the latest portable computers for use in homes by parents as well as students. Because parent learning is so important and learning from the home-school will increase, connections go far beyond the levels of involvement that were considered adequate even recently.

While any parent or caretaker of a student can be a member of the assembly, selecting representatives for the steering committee is tricky, because the parent population is not an administrative or political entity. The parents as a group need to meet regularly (much as a PTA or PTO does traditionally).They need to select representatives to the steering committee. Each neighborhood in the catchment might select a representative that serves on the parent organization leadership team as well.

Businesses and Social Institutions

Representatives of the business community, particularly from the neighborhood to be served, and community library and other relevant institutions need to be included as well—and early.

Some Responsible Parties will represent the federal, state, district, and town or city infrastructure; some will represent institutions or constituents in the neighborhood and immediate community. The idea is to create a governing body that will have legitimacy within the educational organization and with the other entities that have an important interest in the quality of the school.

Educational governance has a purpose—to build the best education possible for the children and emerging young adults of a school or school district. We need to think about the organization of the school and its leadership and decision making from that perspective. The major job of school-level leaders is to examine the state of the school and determine how to improve it. In other words, they must conduct the management of day-to-day operations from an action research perspective, not as a rote routine. Here are the big questions school-based administrators and leaders continuously inquire into—the lens through which they study the health of the organization and determine the effects of their work:

- What are students studying and learning?
- How are they studying and learning? What does instruction look like?
- What social climate are they living in while in our school?

The answers to those questions determine the outcomes of schooling. The higher the quality of what is studied, the more powerful the learning and the longer it endures. The higher quality of the learning experiences students encounter and their engagement with content, the more powerful the learning and the longer it endures. The better the social climate, the more powerful the learning and the longer it endures.

The what, how, and social climate work together to form the trademark character of the school and determine the level of excellence that its students will achieve.

Does a given school need to change to meet the emerging demands and potential of these times? If so, how much? And how? Who makes the important decisions about whether change is needed and, if it is, how to do it? Should standards be set by the federal government? Or by the states? Or ambitious districts? Or individual schools?

There are no simple answers to these enduring questions, but schooling takes place at the school level and each school needs a governance system in which administrators, lead teachers, staff, parents, and relevant community entities are brought together to think about the condition of education and how it might be improved. Such an entity is very important at this time, for fulfilling the promise of the century requires changes that have to be made carefully and understood by the relevant stakeholders.

At the school and district levels, renewal efforts have often failed, either because the changes were too mild or because they were made insignificant by a horde of competing and often underfunded changes. Initiatives have also failed because they attempted to bring about changes too large for schools to make without seriously disrupting operations. We seek an "optimal mismatch," where a change is significantly large to make a difference but is still within the capacity of the organization. The more complex a change, the more stress it places on the organization or a unit within it, such as a team of teachers. We classify changes according to three levels of complexity. Then we try to match those levels to the needs and strengths of the organization and the resources that are brought to bear on the change. We refer to these levels as refinement, renovation, and redesign.

- **Refinement** is modest changes in one or more dimensions of the process of education.
- **Renovation** is a more substantial rethinking and reorganization of a curriculum area or an aspect of teaching or technology.
- **Redesign** involves considerable changes in curriculum and instruction and the relationships between home and school.

Which approach is best depends on a realistic assessment of the capability of the organization. The Responsible Parties need to assess their school's capability and move quickly to plan improvements in promising areas that are within reach. While doing so, they can build up the more powerful modes of professional development and make the changes in the workplace that will enable more complex levels of change. And, optimism is important. Through their optimistic involvement, the leaders of the Responsible Parties can help the members of the school community believe that they can find ways to overcome the impediments that have stymied the efforts of many schools.

In a newsletter early in 2011, Learning Forward submitted to its membership and a wider mailing list an open-ended question asking

- whether the respondents agreed with the concept of the development of hybrid courses;
- how well they believed they were prepared to engage in such development; and
- what kind of help would be most valued.

The response rate was, not surprisingly, low. This was not a formal survey of a targeted sample, so the results are not a firm indication of the population's views. They nonetheless contain some very interesting material. About a fifth of the respondents simply agreed with the concept and indicated that professional development would be welcome and needed. Many of the others did not answer the question directly but dealt with perceived obstacles, particularly lack of monetary resources, lack of technology in their settings, poor present professional development, and poor leadership. Altogether the responses were divided between a minority of optimistic, "let's get going" comments and the discouraged and even somewhat cynical majority.

The respondents were self-selected as well as a small number. Respondents with an obstacle orientation may have seen the survey as an opportunity to express their concerns to someone, somewhere. However, these data should stimulate us to learn much more about how teachers and administrators respond to proposals for development and innovation and their assessment of the current professional context.

Judging from the initial reactions of a proportion of teachers and principals in the settings where we work, strong, integrative, facilitative leadership is needed to develop the socioprofessional communities that can take on the difficult tasks of the near future. In those settings, the initial reaction of a number of teachers and principals to proposals for curricular or technological innovation or for complex professional development is to cite obstacles, but that view is diminished as genuine involvement and real follow-through and facilitation become the norm.

> *Authors' note:* Standards do not a school make. And even the best ones cannot be implemented slavishly and be useful. The school has to use standards as guidelines, but educational environments are made in schools. If a school is self-renewing, with faculty members constantly assessing how it is doing and what needs to change, the environment will be energizing.

To restate—broad, formal involvement of parents, community members, institutions, and businesses is necessary to develop and sustain attempts to improve schooling. Involvement is the key to dealing with the inevitable controversy that accompanies change in any social institution—here, the school. The roles of Responsible Parties are mingled as everyone strives to build a school where personal, social, and academic growth is seamlessly and rigorously promoted. In that school we will see

- intensive, continuous, schoolwide, learning-centered professional development;
- focused school improvement initiatives using an action research format; and
- an energizing school culture.

Essentially, we seek to create what we call a *homeostasis of change*, a condition in which continuous efforts to make the school better are routine. From this perspective, school renewal becomes part of the ordinary process of operating the school rather than a response to a belief that dreadful problems are crying out for immediate solutions. Learning how to do things better and better becomes a way of life, and stakeholders pay considerable attention to creating an environment where the adult caretakers of our children are in a healthy state of study and learning. Creating this evolutionary state is the job of all participants at all levels of the educational system: governmental policy makers, school district leaders and support personnel, and everyone who works in the school. Initiatives from every level need to be informed by insight into the nature of the complex processes of schooling and the complexities of transfusing change into the overall curriculum. Also, initiatives need to address the problem that generated them in the first place. Instead of adding programs for, say, students who cannot read very well, we might strengthen the curriculum in reading so that fewer students fail to learn to read effectively. Both are important.

> *Authors' note:* At this time in history a major school renewal agenda has to include plans for the incorporation or expansion of ICT. A panorama of issues needs to be addressed, ranging from the simplest decisions about basic equipment to whether to infuse ICT throughout every aspect of schooling. We have emphasized democratic process in this chapter, but it is the digital world that is on our minds. ICT will be a major part of Chapter Eleven, where we will present a scenario of a school governed by the Responsible Parties concept.

8 Near-Term Development

Hybrid Instruction and Learning Platforms Near and Far

Literacy has always been the key to self-education—or reception of education, for that matter. Now, the difference between the fully literate, the partially literate, and the strugglers will be monumental and lifelong. If only one core curriculum area is enriched, it should be literacy. Even better that all curriculum areas address literacy and teach beginning and advanced processes in reading and writing.

. . . Our Reflective Observer

Lisa Mueller's first-grade class is studying how to begin a story. They have looked at the first lines of a number of picture/story books and have classified those beginnings (for example, "These begin by having the characters talk about something," and "These begin by describing the main character."). Now, they are watching "TumbleBooks"—online, animated picture books—listening attentively to how the stories begin as the authors of those stories read them.

Soon, each one begins a story based on the beginning of The Sound of Music. *Because they have been studying the devices used by the published writers, many use similar devices as they begin their pieces.*

The unit of study began with print material and then used TumbleBooks to enrich the students' perception of beginnings. Then, film was used to stimulate writing in which the students apply their study of beginnings. They will share their individual writings on the interactive whiteboard.

Writing about education increases our awareness of the many ways school and home are in transition. Our society and government at all levels are trying to face problems that have been long in the making. The inner cities beg for help, and new and serious efforts are being made to provide it, but the journey is still only a few feet down the road with miles to go. ICT is seeping into the school and charging into the home; as things stand, family income largely rules accessibility in both settings. Distance courses and even virtual schools are springing up. Charter schools are being spawned at an increasing rate, and newly formed companies are ready to contract to run them; as solutions, charters vary considerably in quality. Graduation rates in many high schools are frighteningly low, and disparities occur in high school and university education along gender lines. Schooling that once disadvantaged many females is now failing many young males.

In the midst of so much change and so many problems, states, school districts, school faculties, and individual teachers can well wonder, "What should we do now? What should be our priorities? What can we do that will surely pay off for students?"

In these pages we will discuss an avenue that we believe is a very high-probability route to educational improvement, one that will positively affect home/school partnerships and one that will substantively affect the workplace of educators and the quality of professional development. We must develop hybrid courses *now,* at the local school level. We also must begin to adapt the most promising courses developed elsewhere. The 21st-century skills will come alive as instructional hybrids are built.

We recommend that, rather than reinventing the curricular wheel, the Responsible Parties everywhere organize school faculties to build and adapt hybrid courses in the existing curriculum areas. Let's look at what resources such adaptation might involve, then at criteria for development and adaptation, and finally at the activities themselves and the generation of the professional development necessary for the tasks to be feasible and high-quality products likely.

Why begin with existing courses? Because they exist! And, the redevelopment process will not only improve these courses but will help faculties build a base of skills that they can use to design brand-new courses down the line. Existing courses that reflect district, state, and national priorities and standards/benchmarks frameworks are ready to go; these then will form a base from which work can go forward. So let's use them!

Schools and districts have invested widely varying amounts of resource in print libraries and media centers. Now, ICT makes it easy to add massive digital resources, and many schools are doing so. Once these resources are added, faculty can take a careful look at their courses and determine how student inquiry can be enhanced through tasks that connect students to the new resources.

THE HYBRID COURSE

The term *hybrid* refers to campus-based lessons, courses, and curricula where ICT technology is a prominent feature of the design. Sometimes the familiar format of the course is continued, but the vast resources of the New Library provide more avenues for student inquiry. Sometimes virtual laboratories are integrated into the familiar course. Sometimes contact with students in other settings—within and outside of the country—is added. Parts of online courses are sometimes added. For example, the self-instructional and practice components of a self-instructional language course can complement direct instruction in a campus-based language course. Hybrids are not just campus courses where incidental uses of ICT occur. We are talking about serious redevelopment of courses of study with dimensions that utilize the New Libraries and may incorporate elements of distance courses. As time passes, there will be more and better distance courses, many online. And large numbers of our students will take them. We need to ensure that the school is a good platform for them and that homes are supported as they, too, become platforms for learning.

Regarding terms . . . We understand that primary teachers are not accustomed to referring to their lessons and curriculum units as "sets of courses." They may prefer the term *curriculum area*. Both integrated blocks of subjects and single-subject courses can be thought of as courses. (We elaborate on this point later in this chapter.)

Again, when we use *hybrid*, we mean that instruction or other learning experiences are a combination of traditional methods, materials, and artifacts physically present in the classroom with all the resources and Web 2.0 tools that are available online in the digital world. What the combination looks like depends on the desired student outcomes.

For those who are incredulous about attempting hybrid courses for the primary grades, recall that *Sesame Street*—a great distant course—just celebrated its *50th anniversary*. Bruce recalls that about 40 years ago, Bank Street College persuaded Shirley MacLaine and Harry Belafonte to record children's books—about 100 in all—and a special projector turned the pages as they read. This effort brought books to New York children who were rarely read to at home. Mediated study is not new. And, at present, many young children are already journeying through cyberspace.

The early years of *Sesame Street* were carefully studied, and we can see the beginnings of hybrid development in careful evaluation reports spanning more than 40 years (see Ball & Bogatz, 1970; Pasnik, Bates, Brunner, Cervantes, Hupert, Schindel, & Townsend, 2010). Essentially, students learned most when they watched the program with teachers and parents and discussions ensued on the content of the segments. Students did learn when they watched alone, but their achievement was enhanced when either teachers, parents, or both were involved.

The selection of an appropriate model of teaching will be central. Cooperative-inquiry models, such as group investigation, will be essential, as will conceptual models—inductive thinking, concept attainment, scientific inquiry—and divergent-thinking models such as synectics.

Integrating campus resources with digital resources across the grade levels will be remarkably simple. The marvelous New Library is already available, and New Courses are being developed that can be blended with the familiar processes of the classroom. Access to digital resources has alleviated many problems in implementing collaborative/inductive/ inquiry models of teaching. For many years, teachers struggled to find materials to support student inquiry into virtually every topic that was removed from the school by time (history) or distance (other nations). Today, if the curriculum calls for a comparison of life in the home city to life in a faraway culture, teachers have a vast body of available information to draw from. The vast visual collections of libraries make it possible for students to look at pictures and video renditions of places they are studying. Rather than "scrounging," the primary task is now one of "sifting." And, studying their own neighborhoods and communities, they can collect data through cameras, camcorders, and interviews with citizens.

For example, our Charlie has access to virtual reality experiments he can use to extend his inquiry. Tom's class can select a particular region, country, or global problem and get access to data, position papers, and discussions of relevant issues such as population control. Colleagues of ours have favorite sites that help students experience content with greater understanding. In mathematics, for example, the National Library of Virtual Mathematics of Utah State University allows students K–12 to explore math concepts and provides lesson plans and activities (http://nvlm.usu.edu/en/nav/vlibrary.html). While many colleagues working at the elementary and secondary levels use the great Library of Congress digital collections on government, war/military, Native American history, African American history, environment/conservation, and immigration/American expansion (www.loc.gov/), they or the students they work with regularly find new sites, such as Maggie Blanck's "family" site for studying emigration and immigration (http://maggieblanck.com/Immigration.html). Even some of the sites that have a bit of advertising and public relations in them can be useful. An example is www.dairyfarmingtoday.org/, which has segments that provide a useful addition to the study of farming, agriculture, and even conservation. And while some good sites disappear too soon, new sites appear daily.

GIVENS

As we indicated earlier in our brief scenario of the *Alpha* school, the promises involve changing our understanding of resources provided to schools and families. All students, K–12, are provided with laptop computers, smartphones, and appropriate software. The school is open from 6:00 AM to midnight on weekdays and noon to 10:00 PM on weekends. The school library is a branch of the public library. Courses and tutoring for parents are available, and local businesses can also access the resources. Students and their families can access school broadband networks from home. Parents can opt to provide assistance as tutors and paraprofessionals and to administer assessments.

The continuous action research by the Responsible Parties is transparent to the entire community, but privacy for individual students is respected and ensured.

Increasing social, academic, and practical intelligence is a major goal of education. Cooperative inductive inquiry pervades schooling. The 21st-century skills are learned and practiced until they become second nature.

Teachers live the 21st century. Schools are a platform for their learning. About one-quarter of their work time is for their own study and preparation—partly in groups, partly as individuals. Twenty-first-century skills are taught in the core curriculum courses, where they are used in inquiry, rather than in separate ICT courses.

In the envelope of these givens, let's look at the development of courses.

REDEVELOPMENT IS AN ACTION RESEARCH PROCESS: THE NEW MEDIA AND THE NEW MODELS OF TEACHING WORK TOGETHER

As we write, we remind ourselves of a point we made in Chapter Three: Just adding ICT will not necessarily make courses or instruction more powerful. How we teach is critical. We also want to explain again our broad use of the term *course*. The term is familiar in the secondary school where content, staff, and credit are tied to the concept. Less familiar is the application of that concept to the primary grades. It is less common to think of a "course" in reading or writing or the language arts. But, from our perspective, the academic strands of K–3 education are made up of integrated curriculum areas—related "courses." Why do we use the term *course* at all levels? Because we find it useful as we think of the strands of education and how to redevelop them. Thus, in Grade 1 we think of courses as representing dimensions of what, in action, is an integrated curriculum. From this frame of reference, we can redevelop a section of a course on arithmetic and implement it, not just in that course but in the more general curriculum area of language arts.

Clearly, we do not intend that curriculum areas be fragmented by development. Many teachers will prefer to develop an entire curriculum area, such as the language arts, rather than beginning with a section of it. Some teachers, especially at the elementary level, will prefer to develop interdisciplinary units that build language arts, social studies, science, and mathematics knowledge and skill together.

BUILDING THE NEW COURSES ONE AT A TIME

We begin with a series of scenarios in which hybrid courses are developed in the core curriculum areas. These are illustrations, not by any means the only possibilities or even prototypes. Individual teachers and learning communities—thousands of them—will provide examples. Many will also be far more spectacular than these examples, which are modest and well within reach of most schools and teachers.

We believe that locally developed courses will be more valuable than courses imported from elsewhere. The focus of 21st-century professional development is *on* course development. We also believe that states should fund intermediate agencies to provide support and develop examples that can stimulate local development.

SCENARIO: SECONDARY SOCIAL EDUCATION

We return to Tom, whose high school social studies course takes students into statistical databases and other information sources on the nations of the world. The objective is to acquaint the students with the political globe and to help them develop categories of countries, build correlations among various characteristics (as educational levels and religious beliefs with birth rates), and generate inquiries and test hypotheses (Is gender equality related to type of government?). Tom knows that building capacity to inquire inductively builds long-term capacity—academic intelligence. With respect to prior knowledge, Tom has ascertained that only two of his students can look over a political globe without names and correctly locate as many as ten countries, and even these students know very little information about them.

Tom's students have print copies of the State of the World Atlas *(Smith, 2008). Tom has guided them to examine international statistics databases, and, of course, the online* Encyclopedia Britannica *is in their computers. They also have immediate access to Wikipedia (http://en.wikipedia.org/) and the Library of Congress country profiles (http://lcweb2.loc.gov/frd/cs/profiles.html).*

Beginning with simple data sets, he has taught them to build and share categories. He first led them to easy-to-understand variables, such as physical size of countries and populations. Then he facilitated their computation of correlations, teaching them how to cross one variable with another and even how to test for statistical significance. And, he led them to develop hypotheses—"Would size of population be associated with literacy?"—and, using their hypotheses, explore the databases.

Dividing themselves into groups to engage in more in-depth studies of various nations, the students use the encyclopedia and search for books and articles, both in print and online.

Then Tom and his students expand their search about the countries and their cities and institutions. Many of his students are familiar with Google Earth (http://earth.google.com/) but have not used it to understand the geography of the world and its implications. They enjoy navigating and gathering information from the United Nations website, even though some of them think it has a hokey name (http://cyberschoolbus.un.org/). They find the amount of information available in the country profiles of our Library of Congress (http://lcweb2.loc.gov/frd/cs/profiles.html) amazing. Tom's challenge is to help his students inquire into and understand how location of a country can affect its economy, its relations with other countries, and its history and to use this information as they listen to the daily news or read articles in magazines and newspapers and make connections on their own.

Through these searches and follow-up inquiries, students eventually make personal contacts with students in other countries. Exchanges of questions, answers, and pictures follow. Translation programs such as Translator have been an enormous help, as students have entered comments in the class blog (set up through http://kidblog.org/). Tom's students are learning much about the countries they are studying, both how they are similar to the United States and how they are different, as they think about and respond to questions they are asked by students from other countries.

- *Home platform connection:* Tom's course outline is on his laptop and the class webpage, and he writes notes to parents about student progress and what students are expected to do at home. Several parents have asked to attend the class, and they are welcomed.
- *Literacy development:* Tom found it necessary to teach the students a number of terms to help them access and understand information. For example, terms such as per capita domestic product, fertility, infant mortality rate, and literacy levels *needed definitions. He taught ways to compute correlations and averages and built "dummy" tables that his students could use to orga-nize information. Tom estimated that in the course of a semester, he taught about 300 terms, which the students assembled to build a glossary. When students had trouble understanding a term or a passage, they worked online, sometimes individually and sometimes as partners, to determine a word's meaning. For key words related to many concepts, Tom had them complete concept of definition maps (Buehl, 2001; Schwartz & Rafael, 1985). Among other tools, the students have "talking dictionaries" and free online dictionaries*

to help them unlock and pronounce words (e.g., www.merriam-webster .com/). Not all of his students are "digital natives" when it comes to using all the at-hand online reference tools, and many seem relieved at the ease of using multiple online dictionaries as they tap the word in, hear it pronounced, and build meaning for it.

- *Assessment: The continuous formative examination of vocabulary and comprehension enables Tom to adjust the educational diets of his students, providing more application and review of some terms. His advice to them is never to skip over a word without putting in the effort to master it.*

To learn whether the students can apply their new skills and knowledge, Tom uses an assignment, familiar to many teachers, that helps his students apply the knowledge and concepts they are engaging with and allows him to study their performance and facility with the concepts and with ICT skills. Students are asked to learn what it would take to visit another country. They are to learn about transportation costs, accommodations, language, requirements for visas, and, most important, they are to find sources that can help them learn about prevailing attitudes toward American visitors. They will find that State Department publications, newspapers from the countries, and travel guides, most of which are available online, provide information to help them complete the assignment. Imagine that a student was assigned Hong Kong. That student would learn about airfares; whether there are youth hostels and what two-star hotels in Kowloon are like; whether a visa is required; and what the South China Morning Post, *the English-language newspaper, reveals about views of America and Americans.*

Students use print sources available in the school and many online sites. Tom has a list of resources, some of which have been mentioned earlier. Students regularly add new sites. Some of the main ones used in this part of the unit include one on etiquette in other countries (www.cyborlink.com/besite/), the international segment of the U.S. Census Bureau (www.census .gov/population/international/), and several of the links from David Warlick's Landmarks for Schools (http://landmark-project.com/).

Students plan trips for their families, and using what they have learned, they prepare dossiers on their countries and post them on the class blog. (Some students have been embedding their presentations into the blog using Zoho Show [https://show.zoho.com] and are much more facile with it than Tom.)

The 30 students share these assignments in a variety of ways—a popular activity. Tom notes how competently they are able to manage the tasks. Tom's practice fits with the "authentic assessment" frame of reference, in which "school learning" is examined in the context of "real-world" tasks, giving the students the opportunity to exercise their new knowledge in areas of potential practical application.

Tom's students learn individually, with each other, and with students and experts from afar—with Tom facilitating the learning experiences and ensuring that the basic curriculum concepts central to his course are mastered and extended, including skilled ICT use. As we leave Tom and his class, they are creating podcasts to share with parents and other classes. Working individually, each student is also composing a piece addressed to Tom expressing his or her learning during this unit of study.

Commentary

Note that Tom did not simply send the students into the New Library to find information. He polished their inductive skills, both the building of categories and the search for correlations. Within the course, the students worked as a class, in small groups, and as individuals. As they proceeded, Tom scheduled sessions on learning skills and summarizing findings. He helped students address audiences beyond the classroom—parents/caregivers and global contacts—so that students would be impelled to organize and communicate the content.

He also studied what they knew at the beginning of the course, watched their learning progress, and provided a summary task for each individual student.

Tom's Knowledge, Skill, and Professional Development

To build and teach his course, Tom had to master the content and learn what the New Libraries offered and identify some of the best online sites for his students to access. He needed a considerable range of ICT skills and a frame of reference with which to determine those skills his students knew and those where they needed instruction.

Also, note that building basic literacy skills was built into his teaching. To read fluently in the areas being studied, students needed to develop understanding and use of several hundred new words and concepts and learn to use them in writing as well as reading.

A Big Question

Tom could learn how to develop and teach the course on his own or partly in professional learning communities with others with similar needs. The inquiry processes he was teaching are similar across the curriculum. Could the faculty learn these together? Should they?

Through the National Council for the Social Studies, he would find considerable resources and could connect with other teachers and professors with similar interests. Comparable resources are available in all the major curriculum areas.

Another Big Question

To what extent could other teachers adapt Tom's course and use it in their settings? Or, is the development process an important part of the preparation to teach?

A Question About Continuity

While the content of the course is important on its own terms, in the long run, what is most important is to increase students' capacity to learn. To what extent is a course part of a curriculum that addresses standards and benchmarks that can be used to shape the course and assess the outcomes? In Tom's case, he used standards and benchmarks as his starting point but, ultimately, focused on his students' attaining and using higher-order skills.

Long-Term Evaluation

The popular assignment of preparing trips to a number of countries enabled Tom to see how well his students could apply the inquiry mode.

After Tom's students have been in school for another semester or year, he can follow them to determine how well they recall information and concepts. If they take another course with him, he can determine how well they apply the inductive methods he has taught them. Or, his colleagues could determine how well the students apply those skills in their courses. Long-term formative assessment of higher-order skills is a whole-school process because developing those skills takes time—a semester or more—and application in future years is the goal. Nonetheless, the tour-planning project provides a good deal of information about the competence the students are likely to carry with them.

SCENARIO: HIGH SCHOOL BIOLOGY

For development of a hybrid in a companion secondary school subject, let's revisit Nancy Olson and her colleague, Judy Uris, teachers in northern Wisconsin. As well as teaching, each of them supports study groups of secondary and elementary teachers in the area. They have been studying the vast amounts of biological science materials available on the Biological Sciences Curriculum Study (BSCS) and the National Science Teachers Association (NSTA) Learning Center websites and have been redeveloping their courses on general science and biology. Nancy and Judy are particularly taken by the online laboratory simulations that are available in all the sciences at this time. However, they think they have the content well under their own control and can implement effective campus courses while using ICT for several other purposes.

They decide to build hybrid courses with substantial laboratory components and to incorporate a number of simulations that will guide the students to expand their study of various topics and can lead them into more areas for inquiry. In addition, some available online units can serve their students as "tutoring" additions, and the New Library can serve the literacy dimension of their course.

They design the courses using the scientific inquiry and cooperative inductive models of teaching. (Like Tom, they know that inductive inquiry builds capacity.) Topics are introduced in such a way as to generate puzzles that become springboards for inquiry, initiating cycles of group and individual inquiry. Judy and Nancy assemble large collections of live plants that the students will be assigned to tend and have created "greenhouse windows" that face in various directions. Each of them has developed a study that will require the students to collect and analyze data under their guidance. Each unit of the course also contains tasks that open up studies in virtual laboratory conditions.

- *Vocabulary and literacy skills:* Nancy and Judy teach the students ways of organizing data. The students also identify words with which they need extra practice to enhance their sight-reading and on-call writing vocabularies. Judy and Nancy have students build glossaries and test each other's acquisition of words. Students who have problems in the literacy area are referred to a Tier II intervention of the type described in the next section.

- *Assessment:* BSCS courses provide access to content-relevant item banks. Observation of the processes of inquiry is the core of the evaluation. The students complete "authentic" tasks by observing trees and animals in their neighborhoods. The tending of the plants in the teaching laboratory keeps them in touch with the relationship of scientific inquiry to the process of living. In their general science courses, you can bet that Nancy and Judy relate student inquiry within the course to students' lives—as in thinking about day-to-day applications of electricity from a scientific point of view. During the course the students will explore induction, the development of electromagnets, and the design of electric motors. They will then locate the motors in their homes and report on their uses and various designs. Course assignments are posted on the class webpage, and the students can communicate actions, findings, and results on a blog.

Commentary

We should begin with a caveat: Not all courses should automatically become hybrids. But Nancy and Judy are determined to elevate their courses, involve the students in serious inquiry, and have those students apply the science they learn, rather than seeing the sciences as courses to be taken and forgotten.

SCENARIO: MIDDLE SCHOOL COURSES IN LITERATURE, READING, AND WRITING (INCLUDING A TIER II INTERVENTION)

We visit Mary Bishop again. She teaches two yearlong courses in the middle school, one for eighth-grade students who are making average or above-average progression in literacy and one for students who are still struggling with reading and writing. The eighth-grade course is on the Canadian short story, and the textbook is the New Oxford Book of Canadian Short Stories *(Atwood & Weaver, 1995). The course for struggling readers is called "Read to Succeed" and is designed around the Picture Word Inductive Model of teaching (Calhoun, 1999). For struggling older readers, the course is a Tier II intervention in Response to Intervention terms.*

The print medium is important in both courses. Mary's classroom is a library with more than a thousand items at a wide range of levels—from books whose content is conveyed largely by pictures to adult fiction and nonfiction. She makes it clear that one of her major objectives is to have the students analyze a large enough quantity of writing that they will gain access to the "Big Library of the World." Lifelong reading is the major goal.

An interactive whiteboard is used for categorization and analysis.

- *Home platform connection:* Mary's course outline is presented on the class webpage, and progress through the year is posted online. (The school uses Infinite Campus.) She emails comments to parents when she wishes to share observations and invites them to communicate with her as they feel the need. These comments are shared with the student but are otherwise private—available only to parents, the individual student, and Mary.

  In this unit, the print medium is central. When writing, the students will use their laptops and networked printers, but Mary's course does not begin in cyberspace. Her students will enter it when the time comes to access newspapers and libraries and extend their categories.

- *Literacy development:* Without strong literacy skills, students cannot profit from the cyberspace revolution. Mary epitomizes the kind of teaching that is essential if the promise is to be fulfilled. Central literacy skills are nested in the print library and extended to the other dimensions of the New Libraries. Another hybrid environment is created, beginning with face-to-face connections and then increasingly using the New Libraries.

Mary will also visit us later as we develop our theme.

Commentary

Mary builds her courses around important topics in literature and teaches the students how to categorize and how to use categories. In this case, she is determined that students get a better knowledge and appreciation of writing by Canadian women. There is, by the way, a real Mary Bishop who teaches struggling readers and has written five books that have been published for the young adult market.

While the development of hybrid courses tops our agenda of 21st-century school reform initiatives, we are also mindful of the promising reform efforts of recent decades from which we learn and on which we build.

IMPORTANT LITERACY PROGRAMS FOR ELEMENTARY STUDENTS

Here we will describe several prominent curriculum programs that school teams can draw on as they consider their own development activities or adopting the products of others. First, let's look at two programs on reading that accommodate the needs of struggling readers.

Success for All

For more than 20 years, the Success for All literacy curriculum has generated consistent if moderate gains among the most unlikely populations of Title I students. The magnitude of its success is dramatized by the title of the book summarizing the approach and its successes: *2 Million Children* (Slavin, Madden, Chambers, & Haxby, 2009). Success for All asks that schools vote to participate, works within the confines of the usually available time for staff development, provides facilitators with follow-up on their training, and helps schools adjust as they implement the curriculum materials. Effect sizes for a year range between 0.30 and 0.40. Some students gain more in comparison with those in schools not using Success for All. The effort is important for a number of reasons, including that it targets schools in economically poor areas and that the results conflict sharply with the dismal findings from less structured Title I efforts.

Reading Recovery

Reading Recovery is a program for struggling readers in the first grade. Specially trained tutors work with students one-on-one for 30 minutes a day for about 12 to 20 weeks. Evaluating the effects is complex, but we estimate that the program effectively reaches about three-quarters of the students referred to it and the effects apparently persist through elementary school and beyond (see, for example, Pinnell, Lyons, Deford, Bryk, & Seltzer, 1994; Schwartz, 2005).

Now, let's look at the long-term development in biology.

Biological Sciences Curriculum Study (BSCS)

The BSCS curriculum was developed 40 years ago (Schwab, 1965) and is still going strong, with communication among teachers facilitated through the Eisenhower Program and the ICT environment of today. The program is designed to teach the process of science through units in which the students are led through experiments to test or generate knowledge in biology. The instructor ideally has an ongoing study of his or her own going in the classroom and shares progress with the students. BSCS conducted (and still conducts) internal evaluations, which have shown that it achieves its goals.

And, then, there is inductive inquiry in general.

Inductive Inquiry: The Research

Over the years, other inquiry-oriented science and social studies curricula have generated fine student effects (see Bredderman, 1983;

> The durability of BSCS is probably due to its focus on teachers who have much in common—they staff the biology and general science courses in our schools. The manuals and textbooks are designed for the self-training of those instructors, and the summer workshops and other experiences are designed according to the theory-demonstration-practice paradigm that appears to be so effective in helping teachers develop complex skills. The efforts and writings of the late Susan Loucks-Horsley were important in the BSCS movement. The influence of the academic reform movement and research on professional development are combined in many of her books (see, especially, her description in 2003).

El-Nemr, 1979) in content, scientific method, and positive attitudes toward the content. Analytic approaches to the teaching of writing have also done very well for student learning (see Hillocks, 1987). The curriculum models range from very direct ones with specifically defined content and procedures to cooperative learning models and nondirective teaching.

AVENUES OF DEVELOPMENT

Altogether, the times call out for three kinds of development in the content, process, and climate of courses of study:

1. In the near term, considerable energy needs to be devoted to the development of hybrid courses that combine face-to-face teaching, use of ICT resources, and independent study.

2. Concomitantly, cooperative inductive/inquiry approaches to teaching and learning need to be built into those courses. The inquiry processes essential to comprehension and expression can be used in the mathematics, science, and social studies curricula. And learning to teach inductively with integrated ICT needs to be a central part of professional development.

3. Literacy needs to be a major component of the development work in every content area. *Literacy* includes reading and writing, global/cyberknowledge and skill, and literacy in subjects themselves.

Strengthened support of the home and community learning platforms will affect education that occurs there and the quality of living.

We will know we are on the right track when our high school graduation rate passes 95 percent and successful postsecondary education, work placement, or college attendance follows graduation. At those rates, socioeconomic status, ethnicity, race, and gender will no longer affect educational level except in a celebration of our diversity.

9

Crossroads— Actually Cloverleafs—for the High School

Social change has affected the productivity of secondary education and brought new demands. Change will wash through its halls, leaving some familiar features and sweeping others away. Most important, the old institution will be elevated to meet challenges and take advantage of the opportunities presented by the new *libraries,* new *courses, virtual schools, and* new *home/school connections. Renewed professional development is vital.*

. . . Our Optimistic Reflective Observer

Can the secondary school reclaim the dissipated senior year, make literacy a powerful central priority, rebuild campus core courses into hybrids, and generate the vitality to avoid declining into a center for counting online credits? (See Coughlin's [2010] excellent article on this subject.) This is "to be or not to be" time, seriously.

. . . Our Worried Reflective Observer

This chapter begins with a brief history of the American high school and its curriculum, then identifies some serious contemporary problems that need to be solved relatively soon. We conclude with proposed solutions to these problems.

For a century or more, the prototypical high school was an American apple pie vision and in many ways a place for aspirations, if not always for accomplishments. Emerging young adults entered ninth grade, engaged in a four-year curriculum of relatively standard courses, romanced the girl or boy of their dreams, went to work or college, and paddled into the mainstream of adult life. Looking back, many high school graduates recall flirting in hallways, cramming for tests, and being lifted by the strains of Elgar's "Pomp and Circumstance" on graduation day.

Not a bad vision. Perfection was not common. Lots of folks didn't graduate; the graduation rate did not reach 70 percent until 1960. Lots didn't get to colleges they were qualified for because they didn't have the money to attend. Lots went to the altar with neighbors counting the months before the first baby arrived.

This vision of high school has been deeply ingrained in the American psyche. It suggests a clearly defined route to upward mobility and economic and social well-being: get a good job, build a family, and enjoy a loving household.

The high school also did a lot for neighborhoods and communities besides delivering education. It brought together the emerging young adults, taught them to relate productively to one another, gave them a sense of citizenship, launched them into adulthood. In many communities, the auditorium was a town center and a place for gatherings for many purposes, not just the senior play.

CURRICULUM AND THE CARNEGIE UNIT

Between 1890 and 1910, efforts were made to solve problems relative to the transition from high school to college. Individual colleges admitted students through a variety of devices, including estimating students' capacity through an interview process. There was little in the way of standardization: high schools had a variety of curricula, and some graduated students after two, three, or four years of study. (As late as the 1920s, the high school attended by one of our relatives added a fourth year for another student and him so that they could complete the college preparatory program.) The Carnegie Foundation developed the "unit" in 1906 to establish minimum standards for the college preparation unit. A unit was defined as 120 hours of classroom study (about a year of 40- to 60-minute sessions 4 or 5 days per week). Fourteen units were required.

The Carnegie Unit provided a structure of courses in the core curriculum subjects that became the requirements for graduation in the college-preparation track of the high school. Essentially, it codified the core curriculum areas offered in Grades 9 to 12. Put simply, it established the tradition of four yearlong courses in each core area—English literature and writing, mathematics, science, and social studies—and a two-unit requirement in a foreign language. Prodded by the foundation and with the carrot of the pension fund, colleges agreed to consider for admission a student with a high school diploma whose curriculum had included those subjects.

Thus, the Carnegie Unit brought considerable order to the relationship between high school study and college admission. Over the years, states and accreditation agencies added a variety of requirements, particularly in the arts and physical education. The general outline is familiar to nearly everyone who grew up in American culture. The Carnegie Foundation also established a system of pensions for college professors (TIAA-CREF) and offered it to institutions that would accept the Carnegie Units as evidence of qualification for college study. Much of the leverage for the Carnegie Unit's spread was that colleges had to accept it to participate in the TIAA/CREF retirement program for professors; thus, the structure was disseminated through higher education as the standard minimal requirement for admission to colleges and universities.

High school students might take the college preparatory curriculum; a curriculum in vocational education, at that time basic "shop" classes that were preparation for basic carpentry, metalwork, electrical wiring, and such; or a commerce-oriented (commercial) program, which was largely oriented toward the preparation of stenographers and book-keepers. Gradually the vocational and commercial curricula disappeared in many schools, and the academic curriculum or a cut-down version of it became the general curriculum for students who did not aspire to college.

Time and the Carnegie Unit: The Class Schedule

During most of the 20th century, the typical curriculum was based on a six-period day—think of an hourlong period with 50 minutes of class time and 10 minutes to get to the next class. In the 1950s, a student's program for a year might look like this.

Mathematics—ninth grade, Introduction to Algebra; tenth grade, Advanced Algebra; eleventh grade, Geometry and Trigonometry; possibly a business math course

English—four years of classes usually covering an aspect of

> The Carnegie Unit is under attack in some quarters because of the mistaken notion that it requires "seat time." In most districts, students have had the option of independent study, of transferring courses from colleges, of passing the GED, and, today, of substituting online courses.
>
> A new kind of unit needs to be developed that will put a decent floor under secondary school requirements while permitting a great variety of equivalent ways of satisfying them.

literature and attention to writing skill. Students read two or three novels and two or three long plays each year and often an anthology of short fiction, essays, and poems.

Science—ninth grade, General Science; tenth grade, Biology; eleventh and twelfth grade, either Chemistry or Physics as electives or Advanced General Science

Social studies—U.S. History, World or U.S. Geography, or Problems of Democracy

In a six-period calendar in the tenth grade, a typical day might look like this:

8:30: 30-minute study period, often in the "homeroom" where attendance was taken and announcements and logistics dealt with

9:00–3:30: Six periods of about 50 minutes with 10 minutes between them for students to move from class to class; 30 minutes for lunch

The four core subjects were taught every weekday. On some days, students had two periods for what were called "study halls." In this way, time was provided for using the library, completing written homework, or reading recreationally. On alternating days, students had one study hall and another period for art, music, or physical education.

Many courses were structured around textbooks accompanied by supplements, including laboratory manuals, quizzes, tests, and ideas for term papers. The textbooks were designed to provide instruction for about 17 weeks per semester. Commonly they were organized into weekly or monthly "units" complete with review and homework questions. By mid-century, teachers' editions contained detailed manuals, going so far as to include suggested questions around which to build class sessions. Publishers often provided masters for "ditto" and mimeograph machines; these were succeeded by overhead transparencies and computer discs.

Standardized testing grew apace during the 20th century and tended to hold instruction within the parameters of the curriculum. Standardization accelerated with the development of Advanced Placement courses, where students' results on an extensive program of external tests determined whether they earned advanced college credit or not. Because Advanced Placement courses relied on such tests and publishers had to ensure their textbooks covered the material that was tested, they represented an extreme example of standardization. The most common teaching method in high schools was (and continues to be) the *recitation*, where material is read, or a presentation is made, or exercises done and the teacher questions the students—that is, the teacher impels the students to *recite*. The Advanced Placement courses took the recitation to a new level, as teachers were evaluated in terms of the percent of students passing the external tests. Many teachers and administrators did not realize that *conceptual teaching generates higher levels of achievement*, and the companies developing the tests preferred—and still prefer—to measure the simplest content they can get away with.

The tendency to use recitation and the preference for testing lower-order content made high school learning a matter of pushing oneself through the curriculum: read what was assigned, write what was asked, and prepare for tests whose items were not synchronized with the curriculum. (See Chapter Twelve for a discussion of evaluation practices and how to improve them.)

CHANGES IN THE HIGH SCHOOL AND THEIR SIDE EFFECTS

In the last four decades of the 20th century, high schools experienced a series of significant changes. Some of these came about because of policy changes, some because schools themselves adopted new practices, often following normative trends, and some because of technological and social changes. Some of these changes, whatever their benefits, have generated concurrent, usually unanticipated, problems. We will consider the following changes and some of their unanticipated consequences.

- Consolidation and increased school size
- The vanishing study hall
- A bundle of internal changes—more and shorter class periods, more elective courses, and reduced "passing" time
- An unanticipated and serious side effect—the empty senior year
- A casualty—the sense of belonging to a student body
- The increasing age of students

Consolidation and Increased School Size

The movement to consolidate small high schools into larger ones began in earnest following the 1959 publication of James Bryant Conant's book *The American High School*. Conant strongly maintained that small high schools could not match the breadth of offerings of large ones and that their teachers in, say, science had to teach all the sciences whereas in large schools they could concentrate on just one of them.

Many school districts began to consolidate their schools voluntarily. A number of states required that small districts work together to build larger regional high schools. The largest cities had built sizeable secondary schools starting early in the 20th century, and they have continued to do so until recently.

The pendulum of opinion has swung. The larger high schools offered relatively few new courses, which undermined support by disappointing parents and policy makers. Consolidation had some inherent problems. Obviously larger schools were likely to become more impersonal, and obviously students spent more time getting to them. Bus trips of an hour or more each way are not uncommon. And obviously a smaller percentage of students would be able to participate in a variety of activities— theater, glee clubs, orchestras, bands, art shows, and sports. While Conant was promoting consolidation, a careful study by Barker and Gump (1964) identified those and other advantages of the smaller schools. Their findings were disseminated to scholars but were less well-known by policy makers.

Today many voices blame low student achievement, bullying, and low morale on school size. However, size is not the only problem to be faced by secondary schools. Making schools smaller will, by itself, not make as much difference as the current advocates hope—there are other things to do as well. We need to remember that there are some fine large schools and some not-so-fine small schools.

The Vanishing Study Hall

This change came about gradually, mostly during the 1960s and 1970s, and is rarely mentioned today, but it had some corollary effects that are still very much alive. Teachers and administrators did not like to proctor study halls, which often gathered large numbers of students in auditoriums, libraries, or multipurpose spaces with a few teachers watching over them. Also, some educators proposed to increase the menu of courses offered. Gradually study halls disappeared in many settings, and elective courses replaced them.

An immediate effect was to reduce independent study time, which a considerable number of students had used to deal with homework assignments, leaving more to be done at home. That change affected all students but particularly those who needed to work or whose home settings were not optimal for study. These effects continue to the present. If today's students had two periods per day to complete homework, they might experience significant benefits. The changes implemented to fill the time that had been occupied by study halls had other implications as well.

A Bundle of Internal Changes: More and Shorter Class Periods, More Elective Courses, and Reduced "Passing" Time

The amount of time allotted for students to get from one classroom to another at the end of a period—"passing time"—was shortened from about ten minutes in the 1940s to five or six minutes and sometimes less time. The time saved was often used to add another period. Thus, the school began to operate on a seven- or even eight-period day. When lunchtime was squeezed in, all the periods were shortened somewhat. New elective courses were added to the schedule, occupying the periods not needed for the core courses.

We have seen two slightly different patterns when a schedule of eight 45-minute periods is used along with a 7- to 8-hour day (student arrives about 8:00 AM and leaves about 3:15 PM). In one, students take the four core courses, three periods of electives, and one period of physical education and various activities (theater, band, orchestra, glee club, crafts). In the second pattern, one period is still reserved for independent study.

An Unanticipated and Serious Side Effect: The Empty Senior Year

The additional periods led to an interesting pattern. Suppose a student, rather than taking electives or independent study, signed up for an "extra" required core course. Or even two. Students who take online or community college courses as well can pile up the requisites for graduation rapidly. In senior year, a large number of students need to take only one or two courses to finish the requirements for graduation.

What do those students who need only one or two more courses do?

A worst-case scenario is that they take an implicit vacation. These young adults can just "hang out" for a year, with a reduced class load and not much else to do. Unfortunately, this scene has been common (see Kirn, 2010, for a scathing indictment of the "empty, debauched" senior year).

However, there are more positive options.

Taking an elective or two in summer school before senior year would leave the student qualified for graduation.

And, some students go off to college early, and the high school accepts the college credits to fulfill a requirement or two. Some students combine courses in a local community college with their remaining high school courses or just take the remaining courses or their equivalents at a community college. In Florida, about 60,000 students take one or more online courses from the Florida Virtual School or the Virtual Academy. Not all of these are seniors piecing out their program, but some are.

A dreadful consequence is that as more successful students disappear into a half-light senior year or squeeze into college early, less successful students are left without the stimulation of more advanced peers. We are unnerved by proposals to actually do away with the senior year—in one state some legislators, seeing a budget-cutting opportunity, have suggested trimming requirements so that students can graduate after just two years of secondary education. It seems to us that such a proposal halves an already weakened curriculum by dropping the weak senior year rather than revitalizing it, and it may adversely affect the weakest students.

A Casualty: The Sense of Belonging to a Student Body

How much the education experience has changed from a norm where nearly all students entering ninth grade in a school were a "class" whose members took four or five required courses together for four years. The variety of patterns now operating has reduced that consistency. The social climate of the school is extremely important, and the absence of a common educational experience makes it difficult for students to feel that they are working through the curriculum with their peers.

Moreover, in schools where a third of the students are not completing even the truncated requirements, a sense of gloom can be pervasive. In such schools, students frequently have almost no sense of the existence of a real student body, let alone a cohort that marches through high school together.

The Increasing Age of Students

For two reasons the high school students of today are about one and a half years older than were the high school students of the 1940s and 1950s. Adding kindergarten contributed to this change. Prior to the addition of kindergarten, the customary age for admission to the first grade was five to five and a half years. When kindergarten was added, the age set for admission was the same as had been used for the first grade. Consequently, the ages of students in all grades rose about one year. The rationale is that the K–1 students will be more mature and therefore more capable of learning.

Few policy makers looked at the other end of the continuum and realized that high school seniors who were 17 or 18 years old on graduation would now be 18 to 19 years old. They would be "emerging young adults" who want to be treated with dignity and trust. Some of the rules that annoy younger students but do not generate much overt resistance (as rules about gum chewing) are seriously offensive to the young adult.

Probably these young people should have a part in the development of the social ambience of the schools, helping to develop the kinds of norms and regulations that will enable them to flourish and organizing themselves into keepers of a healthy social system.

WHAT TO DO NOW—*RIGHT NOW!*

A considerable change is necessary in the conduct of secondary education. Although many of its deficiencies are not products of technological change, the coming of ICT has exacerbated them. Improving the high school and revitalizing the middle school stand out as a promise of the 21st century. The list of schools' infirmities is large, but the list of solutions is very short.

Here we will identify just four areas where problems in secondary education need to be dealt with *right now* and then offer our suggestions of things Responsible Parties could do in the immediate future. We offer a series of recommendations designed to generate good schools that capitalize on digital technology in campus courses, use distance education effectively, and build a proud and synergistic student body.

Let's begin with a few prescriptions.

Literacy as a Pervasive Priority

We recommend a new curriculum area: the Exceptionally Literate Global Citizen. Made up of substantial courses from Grades 7 through 12, it would be a distinct area (apart from the study of literature) dedicated to several integrated strands of education that need serious attention.

One recommendation is to implement high-level teaching of reading and writing that uses global content as a frequent vehicle. Intensive reading/writing has been a weak strand in most schools—there are *some* outstandingly good literacy programs—and high-level literacy is the key to the good life and the successful life. We propose that the faculty in this area study the advanced teaching of literacy and build hybrid courses linked through the years. This faculty would teach these courses in Grades 7 to 12—we need our best instruction here.

A second recommendation is to bring struggling readers/writers to a high standard. The middle and high schools in most districts give a virtual pass to students who come to them in bad shape—a dangerous practice that should be immediately discontinued. However, we strongly believe that struggling, average, and advanced students must be taught together. Tracking is lethal. Integration by ability benefits the strugglers and does not hurt the best. Presently about 30 percent of students enter the middle and high schools with terrible levels of literacy attainment. We have the curricular and instructional tools to stop the tragic consequences of this deficit. Central to any effort is that our faculty must go to school themselves to study the teaching of reading and writing in all content areas. What aspects of literacy do they need to use in teaching their students how to comprehend and apply the knowledge and skills that comprise their subject?

On the whole, literacy courses need to be taught on campus, but digital energy and resources are very important.

Read to Succeed: A Second Chance to Learn to Read

Here is an example of a promising literacy intervention that we have used. The curriculum was designed to help upper elementary, middle school, and secondary students who are struggling readers. The curriculum is called Read to Succeed. Teachers nominate students from Grades 4 through 12 who are having difficulty in class because their reading competence is poor. The objective is to accelerate their competence, increase their self-esteem, and build their ability to teach themselves.

Teachers volunteer to teach classes of up to 15 students that meet for 90 minutes a day, 5 days a week. The curriculum is designed around the Picture Word Inductive Model (see Chapter Five), which is oriented toward beginning readers. (Keep in mind that regardless of their age, these students are beginning readers.)

The specific procedures include

- the rapid development of sight vocabulary. At first, this comes through the analysis of pictures, as described in Chapter Five.
- the inductive study of words.
- extensive reading at the students' level. And, of course, the teachers read to the students regularly.
- regular writing, largely in response to stimulus material and prompts.
- the study of comprehension strategies with explicit strategy instruction.

Professional Development

In our experience implementing this program in a large number of schools, the major strands of professional development were designed to prepare a cadre of teachers who could offer training and support to the Read to Succeed teachers, to offer continuing training to those teachers, and to build an assessment team that could administer tests of performance in reading.

The cadre was brought together for several days at the beginning of the school year and again for one or two days each month. They were introduced to the curriculum with the theory-demonstration-practice paradigm and worked together as peer coaches. They were assigned to Read to Succeed sections in the schools of greatest need, and the rest of their time was occupied in support of their peers, first cotraining with external consultants and later carrying on all professional development with support from those consultants. They also worked with the consultants to analyze embedded student achievement data collected by the teachers and to synthesize and analyze the formal test data. They summarized it for the administrative cabinet and the board of education and for distribution to the teachers of Read to Succeed and their 53 schools. In June 2006, end-of-year data were available for a random sample of students from 56 sections (477 students altogether).

For the teachers, training is provided during two full-day sessions before school begins followed by eight 3-hour sessions during the school year. The teachers maintain logs in which they record student learning of vocabulary, as well as report problems that need to be addressed in subsequent workshops. During these workshops, teachers are covered by other school personnel or paid substitutes. They share lessons together, peer coach one another, and analyze the results of assessments. They also are prepared to administer the Gray Oral Reading Test (Wiederholt & Bryant, 2001) to assess competence in reading at the beginning and end of the school year. An assessment team made up of the cadre and other teachers and administrators administers the Gray Oral Reading Tests to a random sample of students in each section to provide an estimate of the reliability of tests given by the teachers.

Here are some summative results taken from the report to the central administration and trustees.

Entry and Response to Intervention

On entry to the program, the pretest scores indicate that the average student had made an annual gain of about 0.6 grade level equivalent (GLE) in comprehension and 0.25 in fluency each year; these students were precisely the population Read to Succeed is designed to serve. At each level, the learning history scores are similar—over their years in schools, the entering students had gained at about the rates indicated above, whatever grade they are in, whether they are third grade or eighth grade.

Looking across the entire enrollment, the average gain after a year in Read to Succeed was GLE 1.3 in comprehension and GLE 1.15 in fluency.

However, as is true historically with Read to Succeed, about 30 percent did not gain in their first year in the program. The average gain of the others was GLE 1.7 in comprehension and GLE 1.4 in fluency. In the second year, the 30 percent who gained little in their first year gained at the rate of the other students in the second year. Our belief is that they required a longer time to

(Continued)

(Continued)

develop habits of study and optimism, habits that had fallen into disuse as they had failed to learn for several years before Read to Succeed was initiated.

The 1.7 GLE rate of gain brings most students to a new perspective on school and school achievement. They are now learning at a decent rate and bring better literacy skills and vocabulary to their classes in the core curriculum areas.

Gender

Sixty percent of the enrollment is males. Scores at entry are similar for males and females, but females gain somewhat more, and the small difference is statistically significant. This difference persisted through the first five years of the program, and no explanation has been developed. However, the gains by the males are satisfactory.

Level of Class

Classes of third graders, fourth to sixth graders, sixth to eighth graders, and students above eighth grade all gained about the same GLE amounts on average. The curriculum did not need to be altered to accommodate students of different ages.

Socioeconomic Status

The Read to Succeed curriculum appears to have similar effects in schools serving students from homes at various economic levels. Some of the highest-achieving sections are in schools serving the urban poor. And the sections serving students from higher socioeconomic brackets are doing very well. Similarly, students identified as having mild to moderate learning disabilities, so often linked to socioeconomic status, appear to gain equally with students not so diagnosed (see Joyce, Calhoun, Jutras, & Newlove, 2006).

Our third recommendation is to use the New Library as a major source of reading/writing opportunities. Inquiry-oriented forays would bring the students into contact with the cultures of the world, world geography (a great laboratory for developing graphic as well as verbal skills), and global demographics. In a certain sense we are trying to provide plenty of needed substance to fuel inquiries through which the advanced literacy skills are being learned and applied.

The development of competence in reading will be studied formatively, and students will analyze their progress and work with the faculty to devise ways of improving performance.

The basic digital skills are learned in the context of the course and applied in the course of the inquiry.

How's that for openers? Literacy is the key to the fulfillment of the promises. And, in a student body, it is the tie that binds. Both excellence and equity are at stake.

Cooperative Inquiry Global-Style

Cooperative learning is a building block of the systematic development of collaborative skills and generates a student body whose learners work together cohesively. We favor organizing the students into cooperative groups of four. In the Literacy for Global Citizenship course, the members are selected randomly for maximum heterogeneity. New groups are formed each semester. In other courses, a variety of patterns might be used—friendship groups, project groups, and such. The students are prepared to work together in the type of support system reported by and the kinds of inquiry described by Sharon and Shacher in Israel (1988). (In both cases, high student achievement occurred.) Although the cooperative groups stay together throughout the semester, on occasion, they can be combined to conduct inquiries as an entire class for various purposes.

Develop Hybrid Courses in All Curriculum Areas

Hybrid courses use the best features of face-to-face campus interaction and capitalize on the New Library and available distance offerings. Essentially, faculty will examine each course offering and determine the best mix of campus interaction and digital resources for that course. The tired old textbook is getting a shot in the arm with the appearance of multimedia texts. The good ones will facilitate development significantly.

Build the Home-School Platform Connection

One of the real advantages conferred by the New Library and distance offerings is the support of independent learning. The school itself needs to provide a setting for study well into the evening and to offer courses as needed for parents. Parents and students need to be oriented to the expectation of study in the evenings and weekends and given the tools and access to study. In a real sense, old-fashioned homework becomes an evening and weekend routine, connected to the course offerings. Through email, teachers keep parents aware of the progress of their children, and teachers can raise questions and ask for help from parents.

THE NEW LIBERAL ARTS SECONDARY SCHOOL (COLLEGE)

The best model we know is to envision high schools as liberal arts colleges, where the core curriculum areas are studied through continually updated hybrid courses. All students take the same courses and can be tutored through online courses when needed. A difference from the traditional liberal arts model is the addition of the literacy course with its action research study, by all students and teachers, of progress. Individual schools need to decide the extent to which a distance course can be substituted for an on-campus course for graduation credits. Distance courses, usually online, are now available for just about every subject, and students should have some degree of freedom, but the school should ensure that a "core of the core" of campus courses is studied by everybody during every year. Certainly homeschooling is getting new wheels, and secondary students can take online courses at will. But a face-to-face community of learners is incredibly important for the society and the individual.

Our ideal school will feel like the one described in Chapter Eleven. We need to avoid the kind of scenario described by the "unbundling" group:

> Most material would be presented to students by technical means, but teachers would track students' work and intervene when needed. Consistent with the design of the instructional system, teachers also could suggest enrichment work, design projects, lead discussions, and present material not covered by technical means. (Hill & Johnston, 2010)

The title of the article, "In the Future, Diverse Approaches to Schooling," does not match with the monolithic view of education in the quote. There is not much diversity in proceeding at your own pace through a programmed course.

The best hybrids will incorporate the cooperative/inductive/inquiry complex of approaches to teaching because they will teach needed learning and problem-solving skills, generate the best long-term retention, and build the synergy of learning communities.

A POSITIVE NOTE

As we look forward: Our *new* high school will provide equity and coherence. If all students are prepared for higher education, including graduation in a timely manner, ethnic and racial differences will be greatly reduced, and prosperity and social responsibility will inhabit the lives of all people.

10 The School as a Platform for Professional Development

The Reciprocal Concept

Action research is a rejuvenating way of doing business in education and all other productive enterprises. The backbone of professional development models is an action research cycle: studying the current situation, figuring out how to make it better, taking promising actions, studying the effects of these actions, and continuing the inquiry cycle that renews our work and helps us determine whether the desired effects are being attained.

. . . Our Reflective Observer

Imagine that we want to use the promise of the ICT revolution to generate a nationwide network of inquiring educators—teachers and principals who study the core curriculum areas and study how to implement innovations in content, instructional process, and enrichment of the social climate of schools. Imagine that schools or professional learning communities (PLCs) can communicate throughout the network, providing ideas and asking for support. Suppose that districts and states respond to those requests and provide their ideas. This two-way Internet freeway is what we call the *reciprocal concept of staff development.*

Why should we do this? Let's look at the following scenarios.

NANCY, FOURTH-GRADE TEACHER

Nancy Brenner is a fourth-grade teacher in Callahan School who regularly experiences several levels of the new professional learning system. *She, the principal, and the other members of the leadership team in her school have been studying how to build action research into their way of doing business. They are doing so through a distance offering by Learning Forward, an international organization focused on professionalization in education.*

She and her PLC are building a new hybrid course on the teaching of writing. This community is drawing on distance support related to her membership in the National Council of Teachers of English. They have relied heavily on the New Standards Reading and Writing Grade by Grade *(Resnick & Hampton, 2009) and* Reading and Writing With Understanding: Comprehension in Fourth and Fifth Grades *(Hampton & Resnick, 2009).*

PLC members found the first resource, though it was designed to support teachers of students K–3, very useful in helping them understand the progression of reading and writing development, how the cognitions that support the development of these two components of literacy are similar and different, and how to design instruction using this knowledge to accelerate students' literacy development. They also sincerely appreciated that the authors focused on only three "sensible standards" in reading and three in writing. They are talking with their school's Responsible Parties. They would like to build on the base of student products in this resource to develop a K–5 writing assessment. They think that most of their colleagues would benefit from studying and discussing the annotated student writing samples, bringing writing from their students, using the interactive lesson plan program to develop lessons, and sharing their results in terms of specific changes in student compositions.

The second New Standards resource helped team members integrate reading and writing instruction throughout their content areas. They feel they have a long way to go before they have curricular and instructional comfort and expertise with their interdisciplinary lessons. One team member is more technologically savvy about blogs and wikis than the others. She set up a wiki for the team, and they share some of the lessons they have developed to improve students' writing, especially in focusing and organizing their pieces.

Nancy herself is learning how to use an interactive whiteboard with her students. She has access to support both through Smart Board, the manufacturer, and workshops from the International Society for Technology in Education (ISTE). She had given her students a data set of examples sentences from books, magazines, and web resources the class had used in their current science and social studies work. The students are to classify them, not by content or sentence type but by how the author organized the information for the reader. Students have worked with the data set twice thus far, working individually and then in pairs as they read all the items and began to form one or more categories and identify its attributes. Nancy has the full data set in her computer, and her students are ready to share some of their initial categories on the whiteboard and discuss the attributes and why the author may have presented information a particular way. As they progress through this series of inductive lessons, students will collect sentences from sources they are reading that fit into different categories, test the attributes, and discuss when an author might use one form to structure and connect her ideas instead of another.

As students clarify the attributes of different text structures at the sentence level, Nancy will have them produce examples that relate to their science experiments and social studies work. Students enter many of the items they find or create into a file on one of the class desktops. This makes it easy for Nancy and all the students to use these items on the whiteboard as they test attributes and discuss the utility of a particular way of organizing information. Knowing Nancy, she will also have her students doing mini composing think-alouds to explain why they connected their ideas as they did before they move on to analyzing the structures of longer pieces of text.

Her district central office is concentrating on developing offerings on formative assessment using the work of Popham (2008) and Bailey and Heritage (2008). Nancy's PLC and the Responsible Parties at Callahan think that their work will fit smoothly with the district's focus on formative assessment. But district leadership is wisely taking time with development, and workshops in the district are not yet ready. However, a few resources and videos have been put on the district's intranet. These items address how formative assessment is not a new "program" but is a component of instruction that will help teachers improve their lessons and students improve their learning. Part of what the district staff, their area educational agency consultant, and the school-based professional development providers are grappling with is how to prioritize the curriculum standards and learning progressions so that teachers are not overwhelmed when they begin evaluating their current use of formative assessment and considering changes they need to make.

SALLY, FOURTH-GRADE TEACHER

Sally Henderson, teaching fourth grade in Dublin School, is working on renewal of her credential for teaching children with special needs. She is taking online courses at the state university. Her most urgent professional problem is how to work effectively with her Grades 4 to 6 students who are poor readers. The university does not offer courses in that area, so she is taking a course on how to build productive relationships with parents and increase literacy activity in the home. She is searching for a distance course on curriculum for struggling readers.

BILL, FIFTH-GRADE TEACHER

Bill Natchez, who teaches fifth grade in Williams School, is trying to find ways to assess the competence of his students in mathematics. He is enrolled in the master's program of a consulting firm whose courses are recognized by a local college. The firm doesn't offer courses on the assessment of mathematics, but it does have offerings on qualitative evaluation. It also offers courses on how to prepare students for tests, and Bill has chosen those, partly out of frustration and partly because of pressure from his school to improve test scores. A consultant from the regional agency that serves Bill's school is helping him find a distance offering specifically related to assessment in mathematics.

ALTERNATIVES

We have the opportunity to choose among seriously different alternatives for our future.

In the first case, Nancy teaches in an environment where sets of learning opportunities have been designed to further multiple aspects of professional competence. In the second, Sally has relied on the thin set of distance offerings from her university but is now getting help to find a wider spectrum of offerings. In the third, Bill depends on a large set of offerings available from commercial enterprises and is making do, but he has discovered that most are out-of-date imitations of long-standing workshops. He is now getting much-needed assistance in searching for more courses relevant to his needs. Nancy's costs are modest; she pays just her share of the development costs of the offerings she has selected, while her district picks up the costs of the leadership and PLC workshops. Sally pays a stiff tuition, and Bill's expenses—the equivalent of tuition charged by major universities—are the highest.

WILLPOWER

The learning community model can be as powerful for teachers and their learning as it is for students. On one level, technology provides an opportunity to open up the isolated classroom and to bring in new resources to support teachers. Even more powerfully, communications technology provides opportunities for collaborative learning environments for teachers in which they can reflect on practice with colleagues, share expertise in a distributed knowledge framework, and build a common understanding of new instructional approaches, standards and curriculum. (Riel & Fulton, 2001, p. 522)

Many of us probably agree with the ideas in the paragraph above. But we have shared it to acknowledge that the idea of students working together and using technology and multiple resources to fuel their learning and inquiry and the idea of teachers engaging in similar modes of cooperative learning and inquiry have been around for a while. The ideas presented in this excellent article over ten years ago are still far from being implemented in many schools. We do not lack knowledge but rather the collective leadership and willpower to figure out how to make our schools and classroom centers of inquiry unconstrained by physical walls and lack of resources.

The profession—individual educators, school faculties and Responsible Parties, area education agencies, and state departments of education—needs to take the initiative now. Otherwise, government-led initiatives to improve schools will be dominated by evaluation models that focus on getting rid of presumably poor teachers and schools and neglect the learning that teachers need to get better and model lifelong learning for their students. Many of the distance offerings for professional development are currently dominated by commercial sources and entrepreneurial development by universities and some national organizations. They are not all of equal quality.

The emerging ICT initiatives will provide even more courses, virtual schools, and individualized opportunities for study. However, many of these offerings are oriented toward replacing existing district professional development rather than developing a forward-looking, profession-improving stance or implementing broad concepts of school improvement. On-site professional development, partly in the form of self-development by PLCs, is needed, as are hands-on workshops. We need courses, such as those described in Chapter Nine, that wed curriculum development and implementation to professional development. We need these courses to involve teachers and school-based faculty members in studying their practice, studying our professional knowledge base, identifying areas of need, and working together and with those from afar, both face-to-face and online. Some of this work would be schoolwide, some would be done by small groups such as PLCs or grade-level or disciplinary teams, and some would be done by individuals.

A very important question is how much energy to devote to networking teachers and administrators and how much to give to offering curriculum and instructional alternatives that have promise for improving the learning environment. Networking will provide opportunities for practitioners to share ideas, but these will come from their current practice. Distance offerings that generate innovations in practice will be more complex and will both develop and require peer coaching—usually more intense interaction in PLCs—if implementation is to take place. Probably a balance is the best course of action.

So, what would initiatives to build the nationwide network look like? Here are some foundational principles to build on:

- Schools teach through what they teach, how they teach, and the kind of place they are (their social climate). The content of good professional development addresses one or more of these factors.
- School improvement and good school-based professional development require strong leadership from principals and lead teachers. The most effective initiatives rely on school leadership to learn how to

use them and model implementation, as well as conduct action research where effects on students are studied formatively. Leaders need to organize faculties into study groups where peer coaching occurs as new practices are learned. Advice on leadership that does not deal with content, process, and social climate will not make much difference.

- Essentially, using new content, ways of teaching, and social relations entails increasing one's repertoire to incorporate new practices into the teaching/learning process.

- To learn new repertoire, one must understand it, see it in action, and practice it in the company of one's peers. Demonstrations and instruments for studying student learning are particularly important.

- Distance courses can be developed that include the elements needed to learn new repertoire. They can also prepare teacher leaders and principals to organize the faculty to study and implement new content.

- The initiatives that will make the most difference will be in the core curriculum areas. They will target aspects of those areas that are known to increase student learning when they are the content of professional development.

Authors' note: We can't resist proposing a somewhat more comprehensive vision: Imagine an integrated science, social studies, and mathematics curriculum for Grades K–5 where hybrid courses of study include competence in literacy—reading and writing. In the last few years, less attention has been paid to social studies, science, mathematical concepts, and the teaching of writing than is desirable. As these areas receive more emphasis, an integrated rather than a separate-subjects approach is desirable.

Note that all these areas are curriculum related rather than general principles of teaching, coaching, collaborating. The ultimate goal: a 21st-century elementary school that is web supported, facilitates excellence in literacy, and supports a diverse body of students. Distance professional development can make this happen if faculties are organized to engage in the peer coaching that is necessary for implementation.

THE UNDERLYING PRINCIPLE OF RECIPROCITY

Self-education and *reasonable support* are our bywords. We see these working together in what we call *reciprocal professional development.*

On school campuses, faculties engage in schoolwide action research to improve the learning environment (Calhoun, 1994, 2002, 2004). Teachers working alone or in cooperative study groups develop hybrid curriculum units and courses of study and learn how to use or expand digital applications and resources in instruction.

Curriculum development initiatives create supports for school-based educators. Campus-based groups express needs that guide the development of support entities, both in the form of consultants and distance resources. In many states, county offices and intermediate agencies are in place to provide hands-on assistance, and these need a new focus on professional development.

We see reciprocity as essential. As states develop new curricula (standards and benchmarks), they are obligated to provide the means of supporting educators to implement them. On the other hand, teachers must have the opportunity to express their needs to shape external offerings.

Here we consider how to build integrated staff development services strong enough to handle the demands of the new century. We envision a multidimensional program that brings several approaches to professional development together to support the growth of teachers and other educators. These dimensions are as follows:

- Collaborative, synergistic work
- Colleagues supporting each other through coaching
- Curriculum development

Collaborative, Synergistic Work

Two levels of collaborative work are needed. One is small-group work in PLCs. The other is schoolwide action research in which the entire staff considers the educational program throughout the school and takes steps to improve it.

Schoolwide Action Research

We have learned (see Allen & Calhoun, 1998; Calhoun, 1994) that the development of charter understandings and the processes of collective inquiry call for external support in many cases. We recommend conducting needs assessments of principals and lead teachers who organize schoolwide inquiry. In response, services can be developed and provided to schools through the principals and lead teachers. Some districts operate ongoing "academies" for site leaders to provide such assistance.

Professional Learning Communities

The literature on PLCs is extensive and need not be repeated here (e.g., Hord, 1997; Hord, Roussin, & Sommers, 2009; Hord & Sommers, 2007). The vision is well-known that school faculties are organized into small groups that study the progress of their students and take steps to improve teaching. At this point, such groups clearly vary widely in productivity and satisfaction.

We suggest that there be a continuous survey of the needs of those groups, focusing on what they believe they can accomplish on their own and what kinds of external support they need. For example, we envision that the next few years will see a focus on creating hybrid courses of study that include wide use of the New Libraries and extensive application of ICT skills, trying them out, and revising them. Some groups may feel that they can tackle the development in a given area with their own resources in conjunction with web-based materials. Others may feel that they need help, whether with digital skills or content. As this information is collected, districts, intermediate agencies, and states can provide the needed help in the form of both distance and on-site workshops.

Essentially, we are suggesting that a major function of district and state planning should be to conduct this type of survey of needs and development of support.

Again, for both PLC and school-level inquiry, we emphasize the concept of *reciprocity*: school personnel take responsibility for improvement efforts but articulate their professional development needs to their district, intermediate, and state agencies. In turn, the larger organizations provide appropriate supports to campuses.

Colleagues Supporting Each Other Through Coaching

The funding of lead teachers who can "coach" their colleagues, adding a personal-service dimension to development, has become widespread. Principals implement such instructional leadership programs to provide another dimension of support.

In this area also, we recommend that the larger organizations survey the needs of teachers *and* coaches and deliver professional development supports that are tailored to these needs. And, as schools and PLCs express their needs, the coaches (and principals) are likely candidates to help their colleagues. In other words, if certain needs arise with respect to building hybrid courses in a given curriculum area, the district can prepare the coaches to respond.

Currently there is as great variation in the ability of coaches to provide services as there is in the ability of PLCs to manage their own development needs without help. District and state agencies must strive to reduce that variability. Assessing their needs and responding to them is a direct way to accomplish that. When staff provide service and express needs, the organization should reciprocate by trying to meet those needs.

Curriculum Development

In recent years, the PLC and coaching models have emphasized drawing on the existing repertoires of teachers to fuel study groups and personal service. ICT will combine with the desire for more rigorous curricula to create situations where these current repertoires will not suffice. States, intermediate service agency units, and districts need to develop providers who can lead teachers, coaches, and principals to create and master new or expanded repertoires.

We can see this effort being relatively simple, as when districts provide interactive whiteboards to their teachers. The UK did that some years ago at significant cost and has discovered that many are used only as elaborate "black or white boards." Yet, the device has tremendous promise. Where people need external help, it should be available.

Likewise, as states and districts try to improve and implement standards and benchmarks, they create needs that should be reciprocated. Again, surveys using online tools such as SurveyMonkey and face-to-face gathering of information from Responsible Parties, PLCs, coaches, and principals should identify priority areas, and the help that is needed should be made available.

THE GROWING PLATFORM

In the next few years, much growth will come from the developmental activity of individuals, small groups, and schoolwide action research. As school districts have cut their curriculum staffs, they have depleted much-needed resources, which need to be restored. As states and districts develop and adopt new standards and benchmarks, reciprocal professional development needs to be designed and delivered.

The demands of the 21st century are such that a strong, integrated envelope of learning opportunities needs to be provided to and within each school. Everyone is going to learn new things—developing the hybrid courses of study will propel on-the-job learning to levels we have never seen. We need to draw on the available models of professional development to create a many-sided program that enables teachers to flourish on behalf of their students.

In the next chapter, we'll look more closely at the collaborative, synergistic dimension; the coaching dimension; and the curriculum-development dimension.

Part III

The New Basics of Embedded School Reform

Responsible Parties, Watching Learning Grow, Research and Development

> *We can't just stand still and let technology wash over us like a rejuvenating spa experience. If we stand still, it will just puddle around us. This century begins with a call to make a serious effort to change how we conduct education so that our kids will have what they deserve—an excellent beginning.*

> . . . Our Reflective Observer

The next three chapters deal with several aspects of the school improvement process. Chapter Eleven offers a scenario of a K–8 school where the Responsible Parties are bringing ICT and inductive teaching into reality for students, teachers, parents, and community. Chapter Twelve explores the rationale for moving to formative assessment at all levels and changing from norm-referenced to performance-based instruments of assessment. Chapter Thirteen takes us into the literature and the very limited research on school reform and ICT-enhanced instruction.

11 Pembroke Elementary School

The amazing thing about the best schools today is that they have retained some of the best things done in the past but they are not stuck in tradition. Folks who haven't visited a school for a while will hardly recognize some aspects of these schools. But they will surely recognize the best of what they experienced when they were in school.

... Our Reflective Observer

Place Pembroke halfway between the town center and the suburbs of Camden, a 150-year-old industrial city of about 50,000 people somewhere in the heartland of America. Camden's 20 schools serve about 10,000 students. The district contains 3 high schools, 3 middle schools, and 14 elementary schools. The city's economy has a diverse basis, but employment is somewhat under 90 percent as this story unfolds.

Pembroke serves 600 students in Grades PreK–6 with a staff of 23 teachers, a principal, 10 full-time aides (half paid for by business partners), and 2 full-time secretaries. Three of the teachers are designated as "team leaders" and are paid at the rate assistant principals receive in the district. Included on staff are two teachers who serve the "profoundly deaf" elementary students of the district (an area, incidentally, where technology is enabling remarkable access to learning).

English is the second language for 120 students. Sixty of those students have parents who migrated from Mexico. The parents of many of the other 60 are from South Korea. A state multicultural/bilingual initiative pays part of the salaries of four teachers. In most of the Pembroke households, all parents and adult partners work. About 10 percent of the households operate small businesses in the neighborhood. In about 20 percent of the other homes, one of the parents works in a highly skilled occupation. Twenty-five percent are single-natural-parent households, and in half of those, two adults are in residence. Of the Pembroke students, 40 percent qualify for subsidized lunches under current guidelines.

Pembroke has two grants. One, from a local foundation, provides $25,000 per year to support "women in science and mathematics," an interest of the patrons of the foundation. The state Department for the Arts and Humanities contributes $25,000 to support an "artists in residence" experimental program.

State funds support a number of offerings for adults. The local community college offers a variety of courses on the Pembroke campus, some campus based, some hybrids, and some online. The state university has online offerings for the staff, and two campus-based courses are scheduled, each for six Friday-afternoon/Saturday-morning sessions. One focuses on the teaching of writing and the other on ICT applications for course design and development.

All instructional areas have interactive whiteboards and attendant software and bases. All students are supplied with laptops and smartphones, and the laptops are equipped to receive ebooks. Infinite Campus is installed, and parents are provided with the instruction to use it, browse the web, and use ebooks. Programs for beginners in English are available, as are talking dictionaries in English as well as English-Korean and English-Spanish translations.

THE SCHOOL BUILDING

The structure was built in the late 1920s, when it seems like all the school districts in the entire United States used the same architect. When constructed, the building had 2 stories of 12 classrooms each—each floor an essential replica of the other. The original first-floor plan was a typical "egg-crate" layout with classrooms around wide halls. However, extensive remodeling has taken place, resulting in large learning/teaching areas with sound-baffle bulletin boards that can be moved to reconfigure the space. Small-group—up to 15-person—seminar rooms are tucked away here and there.

THE WORKING SCHOOL

Let's visit the school in operation. We'll start by watching some teaching/learning episodes. Then we'll visit with the Responsible Parties, the governance group of the school. Finally, we'll follow a team of teachers through a day. You will notice that some aspects of the operation are just as they might have been years ago, some resemble the typical school of today with the influence of ICT clearly visible, and some forecast the future. Two of our primary informants are Christine, the principal, and Harvey, the deputy and leader of one of the teaching teams.

To begin, we'll watch some parts of the first day of school for six-year-old kids. Let's step inside and see what's going on.

SCENE I: SIX-YEAR-OLDS START THEIR INQUIRIES

In one first-grade classroom, the children are gathered around a table on which is a candle and a jar. The teacher, Jackie Wiseman, lights the candle and, after it has burned brightly for a minute or two, places the jar carefully over the candle. It grows dim, flickers, and goes out. Then she produces another candle and a larger jar, and the exercise is repeated. The candle goes out, but more slowly. Jackie produces two more candles and jars of different sizes. She lights the candles and places the jars over them, and the flames slowly go out.

"Now, we're going to develop some ideas about what has just happened," she says. "I want you to ask me questions about those candles and jars and what you just observed." The students begin. She gently helps them rephrase their questions or plan experiments. When one asks, "Would the candles burn longer with an even bigger jar"? Jackie responds, "How might we find out?" Periodically, she will ask them to dictate to her what they know and questions they have and write what they say on an electronic interactive whiteboard. Their own words will be the content of their first study of reading.

Next door, children are seated in pairs. In front of them is a pile of small objects. Each pair of children also has a magnet. Their teacher, Jan Fisher, smiles at them and explains that the "U-shaped" object is called a magnet. "We're going to find out something about this thing we call a magnet. We'll begin by finding out what it does when it's held close to different things. So, I want you to explore with your magnet. Find out what happens when you bring it close to or touch the things in front of you with it. And sort the objects according to what happens."

Jackie

Jackie is beginning her year with the model of teaching we call "inquiry training" (see Joyce et al., 2009). The model begins by having the students encounter what will be, to them, a puzzling situation. Then, by asking questions and conducting experiments, they build ideas and test them. Jackie will study their inquiry and plan the next series of activities to build a community that can work together to explore the world.

Jan

Jan has begun with the model we call "inductive thinking." That model (see Joyce & Calhoun, 1998, for a complete treatment) begins by presenting the students with information or having them collect information and then having them engage in classifying. As students develop categories, in this case objects according to how they respond to what the students will eventually learn to call a magnetic field, they will build hypotheses to test. Jan will study how they think and what they see and don't see, and she will help them learn to attack other areas as a community of inductive thinkers.

Note that without hands-on experience, virtual-reality encounters with magnetic force may be misleading. Armed with the hands-on knowledge, Jan's students head for the Internet to see what else they can learn about magnetism.

Behind the Scenes

Several aspects of the Pembroke approach to schooling underlie the ways in which Jackie and Jan are leading the students:

- The overarching curricular and instructional approach will be disciplined inductive inquiry. The students will be responsible for working together to discover knowledge and skills and master them. The cooperative inquiry mode of learning will be taught explicitly, as will the social climate of the teaching/learning relationship. We have watched these kids get their first lessons in learning how to learn.

- Listening, speaking, reading, writing, and viewing will be taught as tightly integrated skills. From the beginning, the students will generate ideas that will be put down in words, and they will learn to summarize and synthesize findings. Initially they will dictate the words; eventually they will key them into their computers and compose ideas about them, either on paper or using a computer. As they learn to read, they will study how authors write and use what they learn to enhance their own writing. This type of approach has been found to generate greater student learning than "following-the-textbook" approaches to teaching the language arts and other subjects (Calhoun, 1997; Hillocks, 1987; Joyce & Calhoun, 1996; Joyce, Weil, & Calhoun, 2009). Importantly, learning technology will be pervasive.

- The school will ensure that all students can productively access the big library of the Internet and can use computers to organize information and express themselves. Online courses will be accessible as well.

- The curriculum in science (and, as we will see, the other subject areas) is fully integrated with the teaching of reading and writing because the instructional models make it easy to integrate these subjects. As the students construct inquiries in science, they engage in a great deal of reading and writing.

- With their colleagues, Jan and Jackie have pursued the study of teaching intensively through the Pembroke professional development program, where they are leaders of professional study groups (similar to professional learning communities). They have examined research on curriculum and teaching and studied effective models of teaching and learned to use them effectively. On this first day of school, the entire staff is making statements to the students in behavioral terms—they are showing the kids the kind of place this school is.

The models of teaching Jan and Jackie are using are familiar in the literature and are in use in many schools today—but not in all of them. These teachers have had extensive training, either self-administered with the help of DVD demonstrations, through distance workshops and courses, or in on-campus offerings. Now we turn to another classroom, one that draws on research on cooperative learning (see, for example, Bonsangue, 1993). A week into the school year, we walk upstairs to see what the upper-grade kids are doing.

SCENARIO II: FIFTH- AND SIXTH-GRADE STUDENTS ACCESS THE WORLD

We pause for a minute at the Creativity Center on the north end of the second floor. The place is crammed with materials, computers, touch-screen monitors and interactive whiteboards, desks for teachers, and a large work area where a local graphic artist and two aides, both students at the local college, are developing materials for an upper-grade world culture and global literacy unit. One of the aides is setting up a PowerPoint presentation of messages from children from several schools around the world to whom the upper-grade students have been writing. So far, the class blog does not have a lot of responses, but they have already Skyped with a class in Nottingham, England.

We make our way to Debbie Psychoyos's fifth- and sixth-grade group, who have been studying demographic data on the nations of the world using an online database. Students were amazed at the different information they found in response to a seemingly simple inquiry: the number of countries in the world. They found that numbers ranged from 195 to 257, depending on the source. They decided the weight of evidence supported 196.

Each of the nine groups of four students have analyzed the data on about 20 nations and searched for correlations among the following variables: population, per capita gross national product, birth rate, life expectancy, education, health care services, industrial base, agricultural production, transportation systems, foreign debt, balance of payments, women's rights, and natural resources. The kids are not novices at this kind of analysis—last year they conducted a similar inquiry into the United States.

The groups reported, and what had begun as a purely academic exercise has engaged the students fully.

- *"People born in some countries have a life expectancy 20 years less than folks in other countries."*
- *"We didn't find a relationship between levels of education and per capita wealth!"*

- *"Some rich countries spend more on military facilities and personnel than some large poor ones spend on health care!"*
- *"Women's rights don't correlate with type of government. Some democracies are less liberal than some dictatorships!"*
- *"Some little countries are relatively wealthy because of commerce and industry. Some others just have one mineral that is valuable."*
- *"The United States owes other countries an awful lot of money."*

The time is ripe for group investigation (for descriptions, see Joyce et al., 2009; Sharan & Shachar, 1998). Ms. Psychoyos carefully guides the students in recording their reactions to the data. They decide to bring together the data on all the countries and find out if the conclusions the groups are coming to will hold over the entire data set. They also decide that they need to find a way of getting in-depth information about selected countries to flesh out their statistical data. But which countries? Will they try to test hypotheses?

One student wonders aloud about world organizations and how they relate to the social situation of the world. The student has heard of the United Nations and UNESCO but is vague about how they function. One has heard about the Organization for Economic and Cultural Development, but the others have not. Several have heard of NATO but are not sure how it operates. Several wonder about the European Economic Community. Several wonder about India and China as growing economic powers.

Clearly, deciding priorities for the inquiry will not be easy. However, the conditions for group investigation are present. The students are puzzled. They react differently to the various questions. They need information, and information sources are available. Ms. Psychoyos smiles at all the furrowed brows. "Let's get organized. There is information we all need, and let's start with that. Decide what you are going to add from today's work to your group wiki. Tomorrow we'll prioritize our questions and divide the labor to get the information we need."

Debbie

Watching Debbie and the students, we can see the same elements of curriculum, teaching, and social climate that we observed last week in Jan's and Jackie's classrooms:

- *Again, a community of learners is engaging in disciplined inquiry.*
- *Reading and writing are prominent.*
- *The curriculum is integrated fully and naturally, again because the approach to teaching how to learn centers on cooperative inquiry and the natural blending of information from various sources. Learning in mathematics is prominent, given the nature of the data to be managed. Science is also important, as the environment is studied in relation to the nations of the world.*
- *Debbie, Jan and Jackie, and their colleagues are studying curriculum and teaching and how to build the social climate of a school. Their professional development program lives in how they study and teach.*

Meeting the Responsible Parties

Now, let's continue our inquiry by trying to find out how this school came to be and how it governs itself.

Let's pay the school another visit on the following Thursday evening and sit in on a meeting of the executive committee of the Responsible Parties, essentially the governing board of Pembroke.

SCENARIO III: RECIPROCITY AND DEMOCRACY ABOUND

Learning Resources Center

Harvey meets us and suggests that we have a look at the Learning Resources Center at the north end of the first floor because it will help us understand one of the agenda items. We learn that the school is open until 9:00 PM each weekday and during weekend hours as well. Parents and other community members use the computers in the Learning Resources Center in various ways, and several small local businesses use them for accounting and other purposes. Reciprocally, the businesses are "business partners" with the school and, among other things, sponsor courses in technology, tax preparation, and other relevant subjects. We remember that several businesses sponsor paid aides.

The Learning Resources personnel work in shifts to cover the hours the school is open. They fill three roles: maintaining the center, providing assistance to users, and providing security during the school's extended hours.

Inside the Learning Resources Center, we find a collection of print books as well as computers that are Internet-ready and equipped with business applications. The book collection is large for an elementary school, and we learn that the Learning Resource Center is also a branch of the city library.

We have a lot of questions about how so many innovations have occurred in one school, but Harvey hurries us to the meeting. "We really try to keep meetings in bounds with respect to time. As it is, the teachers on the executive committee work somewhat nonstandard hours so they can cover meetings without killing themselves. District board meetings can be long and emotionally grueling, and that is the only model some of the parents and teachers have, so we have had to learn how to run amicable, productive meetings. Christine took a lot of training on the subject and conducts a lot of short workshops for the Responsible Parties, the staff, and parents. Some business partners use her for their staffs, too."

Adult ESL Class

On the way down the hall to Seminar Room 1, we notice that there is an adult ESL class in one of the multimedia classrooms. About 20 of the Korean parents are present. All have laptop computers with access to iGoogle—a free translation website featuring more than 50 languages, including Korean, that enables them to write in their native language and get rough translations. Programs for initial English language self-instruction are available, as well as English/Korean translation programs and English-language talking dictionaries. The course provides opportunities to practice common tasks, such as shopping, and the attendant words and phrases with which to accomplish those tasks. We will find out later that oral language use and reading and writing are taught simultaneously and by methods remarkably similar to those that are being used with the children (for a thorough discussion, see Calhoun, 1997, 1999). We'll also learn that much of the content these parents and other community members study is an introduction to American culture and society and how to live here successfully. A major help is a weekly Skype call to a school in Korea when parents can ask questions in Korean and clarify both information and perceptions.

Literacy Celebrated

We also notice a large world map on one section of the hall, colored to portray cultural and linguistic patterns. On a large TV screen, a slide show displays pictures of streets and markets in all the countries of the world—an ongoing pictorial tour. A big chart on another wall, labeled "Just Read: We are a culture of readers," depicts the number of books various groups of students have read independently thus far in this term of the school year. We note that the section of the chart for kindergarten children's records includes books that parents or other caretakers have read to the children. The chart includes markers for goals. Apparently there is a celebration every 10,000 books. A headline on the chart indicates that the 600 children read 70,000 books the previous year.

Executive Committee

Once inside Seminar Room 1, we are introduced to 14 people, about equally men and women. Four people are liaisons: one with the business partners' association; one with the central office of the school district; another with city agencies, including recreation and libraries; and one with media and communications agencies, including the local commercial and public television stations, cable company, and one of the telecommunications companies. Four are parents. The neighborhood is divided into 12 sections, and the community members in each section have elected 2 members of the Responsible Parties or 24 altogether. These 24 have elected the 4 parents we meet—the members of the executive committee. All 20 teachers in the school are members of the Responsible Parties, and they have elected 4 members of the executive committee. The other two are the principal, Christine Jurenka, and Harvey Thompson, one of the team leaders, elected by his peers. We learn that Christine and Harvey are not voting members. We will also learn that the charter—the governance understandings made by the faculty and the Responsible Parties (see Glickman, 1993)—is such that final votes on important issues are made by the entire Responsible Parties group; the executive committee studies options and winnows them down to those the larger group votes on.

We also learn that Pembroke is operated in an ongoing action research mode (see Calhoun, 1994) so that data are collected and research is studied before options are selected; then actions taken in important areas are studied as to their effects and reviewed in terms of their success. Decisions at Pembroke are made in a data-rich environment.

The voteless Christine chairs the meetings, and Harvey is the recorder. There are three items on the agenda, shown below, which was sent out via email a week earlier.

Agenda

1. Orientation of new parents and teachers and elections

We have 83 new parents and 2 new teachers. We have to orient them. In addition, half the Responsible Parties have to be elected, so the neighborhood clusters have to arrange their meetings and conduct the elections. You will remember that these are two-year terms without reelection, although retiring members can continue to serve on committees and are urged to do so.

2. Technology

The business partners and communications partners have an interesting idea to present for initial discussion.

3. Creation of agenda for a full Responsible Parties meeting next week and the community meeting the following week

Data on the summer term are partially analyzed and are a possibility. Just Read needs early attention, as does the bilingual program. The surveys will net some issues to discuss.

Christine reminds everyone that meetings are limited to 90 minutes. "That's so we don't get into the mess our school board sometimes is mired in, where most decisions are made after everyone is exhausted and frustrated," she says in an aside to us.

Planning Meetings and Elections

Christine begins by having the agenda approved—a couple of announcement-type items had been added to it via email—and then introduces the orientation/election agenda item. A subcommittee proposes a series of meetings in the neighborhood "sections" to orient parents to the school, the governance charter, and the election procedures. With some minor changes, the plan is approved for presentation at next week's meeting, along with a plan for dividing the labor; two or three Responsible Parties will conduct each meeting. The first newsletter of the term will advertise the meetings and include a copy of the charter and a description of the election procedures.

Technology Proposal

Christine then introduces Don Duncanson, from the cable system, and Jacqueline Towers, from the school's telephone and Internet provider, who will, with Nancy Targus, manager of the local outlet of a chain department store, make a proposal. Nancy begins: "You all know that the business partners have worked with the school extensively in the area of technology. Many people thought it was very bold when the decision was made to put the bulk of the technology monies into high-quality laptop computers that could be moved easily from classroom to classroom and be provided to students and parents. We had to get special permission from the district office (a nod to the district liaison), and many school board members thought those computers would just walk away. But—they let us do it, and it worked. All told, only 12 of the 700 computers have been damaged.

"The classroom workstations have worked well, and the Learning Resources Center is in good shape. Classes can operate where all the kids have access to databases and online resources. The iGoogle language translation sites are a boon to the bilingual program."

Several hands went up and Christine spoke quickly. "Yes, the bilingual program will be a major topic this year, but let's stay with technology for the moment." Everybody laughed and the hands went down.

Nancy continued. "Thanks, Chris. By the way, concerned folks, technology may be a big help to us in that area. However, moving right along, here is our problem.

"We can now choose from an enormous number of online courses, distance courses that use packages of materials, ebooks including textbooks, and packages of resources relevant to many of the topics commonly taught in schools. Many complicated options for learning are developing. Increasingly our students can take courses we don't offer, can review our courses by taking an online offering, and, soon, might even take a course we offer but not from us.

"Now, Pembroke uses cyberspace—digital technology—in many ways at present, but offering the option of online courses is just beginning to be feasible. And, just this week we learned about a new online library resource that may have even more implications than the current online and multimedia-based courses. PBS has announced the launch of a new 'Digital Learning Laboratory.' It will be an online repository of digital media from public broadcasting services throughout the country. It will include video, audio, images, games, and interactive simulations designed specifically for classroom use. We need to get on top of things—learn what is available and how we can exploit these remarkable developments."

Discussion ensues. Some members worry about quality control. Some are very excited. Some want to know how the teachers feel about having distance courses as a real option that replaces face-to-face instruction. Some wonder how much help students need to profit from these new modalities.

After a while, Christine indicates that five minutes remain. Nancy says, "Well, there is no need for urgent decisions. But I would like your permission to get together a group to study this, including surveying what is out there already and locating scholars who may be studying the subject." Consensus is reached comfortably.

As we left, we asked Christine if they used videoconferencing, Go-To-Meeting, or anything other than face-to-face meetings. She said that usually at the beginning of the school year, most of their meetings were face-to-face and much communication was via email and some by telephone and snail-mail. As the year progressed, more work was done at a distance, and more print communication was done through the executive committee wiki. However, thus far, they continue to have a good number of face-to-face meetings to build community and increase understanding and support for the work of the school.

How It Started

For Pembroke, the trek toward a democratic process began five years ago, when Christine became principal and discovered that the parents and staff were upset because a district plan would send the neighborhood kids on buses all over the district to satisfy a court case alleging that segregation by neighborhood disadvantaged minority students. Christine brought together the business partners and began the collective process we have just observed in microcosm. The community, once organized, persuaded the district, the courts, and the state that it would create a fine school that would both serve and benefit from its polyglot neighborhood.

SCHOOL AND HOME

The Pembroke scenario represents four aspects of the attempt to fulfill the promise of our time:

1. The governance mode brings school, home, and community into partnership on behalf of everybody—adults as well as children.

2. Everyone—adults and children—is in a state of learning. The school brings parents and community members into the learning process for themselves as well as for the students.

3. Educators seize opportunities for continuous improvement in the curriculum areas. Development is not just a matter of finding uses for ICT. But ICT is a major factor, and home and school are brought together more easily because of the ease of communication, the Infinite Campus program, and the fact that all stakeholders work together to improve education and develop skills.

4. The redevelopment of education is at the center of professional learning. Rather than work from a position that new learning is only a response to a deficit or defect, the school builds the pursuit of excellence into its ethos. Like top athletes and scholars, educators at Pembroke find striving for high quality to be normal and comfortable.

Most of what educators at Pembroke are doing at present does not use exotic ICT. However, Pembroke has broad-based governance and has made continuous, incremental school improvement a way of doing business.

12 Direct, Performance-Based, Formative Assessment

Watching Learning Grow

Formative evaluation and action research walk hand in hand. Gain is the key—gain in knowledge, skill, and attitude.

. . . Our Reflective Observer

We emphasize again that the incorporation of more ICT technology is not the only change that will fulfill the promise of the 21st century. Further, many aspects of the technology will not find education to be a hospitable home unless several dimensions of educational practice are changed. A vastly enlarged and focused professional development is one of them. The development of hybrid courses of study is another. For teachers, formative study of progress provides information to use to shape the learning environment. For students, knowledge of progress helps them celebrate growth and understand whether they need to modify their learning strategies.

FORMATIVE AND SUMMATIVE ASSESSMENT

The legacy of Benjamin Bloom is very relevant to realizing the promise of 21st-century education. Since the appearance of the *Handbook of Formative and Summative Evaluation of Student Learning* (Bloom, Hastings, & Madaus, 1971), the distinction between the two types of assessment has been well known by educators, yet the summative variety still dominates. Similarly, despite the innovation of performance-based measures, high-inference, norm-referenced tests are usual. Performance-based formative assessment is the undernourished child we now seek to bring to health and, even, dominance.

The essence of formative assessment lies in its frame of reference—watching learning grow so that progress can be celebrated and adjustments can be made. Students need to have a picture of what they are learning and how much, and they need that picture to be updated at frequent intervals. Teachers need those pictures in order to assess the impact of their instruction and to determine what to change and what to continue.

Classroom teachers need to continuously take stock of learning. So they can ensure that the students are clear about what they are learning and so that procedures can be adjusted in light of progress or lack of it. For example, when teaching a skill (think of something like introducing students to addition of fractions), a teacher may begin by modeling the skill, followed by explaining what she has done. By the end of a week of class sessions devoted to modeling and explaining, the opportunity for practice is provided. At that point, we can see how the students perform. We can also ask them to describe their mental processes when performing. Immediately teachers and students get the good news and the bad—they can determine the degree of mastery achieved. Based on that information about performance, teachers can decide whether more explanation or modeling is needed. Students can keep journals where objectives, procedures, and results are recorded on their computers or other devices. Thus, they can keep aware of purpose, process, and outcomes—and share these with parents.

The principle of formative assessment also applies to school improvement. Schools, districts, states, and the federal government all design initiatives to support and improve education. Those efforts need to be accompanied by action research to determine their impact, again on an ongoing basis. Intervals between data collection need to be much shorter than is often thought, but time, effort, and money can easily be wasted if the extent of intended changes is not documented and their effects understood. The history of school improvement is littered with well-intended initiatives that were launched with fanfare but whose progress was not determined regularly. Then a summative picture revealed that little had been accomplished or, worse, that not much had been done. We need to keep in mind that changes in curriculum and instruction will have relatively immediate effects when that change can improve student learning. However, if desired improvement does not happen within a few months, certainly within the first year, it will not happen later!

We unabashedly recommend that performance-based formative evaluation become the majority practice at all levels. And, while doing so, we must make changes in four aspects of assessment as it is generally practiced:

- Evaluation in education in the United States has focused on periodic summative evaluation. This is particularly true of federal, state, and district initiatives, but it is also common at the school level. Many courses are assessed at the end of term or marking period rather than at short intervals and lack the regular, immediate data gathering that characterizes formative study.

- Formal tests have been oriented toward comparison—toward "norm referencing"—rather than toward performance. Mass-administered, once-a-year, multiple-choice tests are most common, yet these have little diagnostic value. The focus needs to be turned toward performance.

- Gains in student learning are rarely calculated. Course grades are often based on summative, end-of-course assessments rather than the difference between initial and final achievement—the gain. To calculate gain requires taking repeated measures—essentially collecting formative information. Assessing learning at the beginning of the year or course can help educators serve students entering with high and low levels of knowledge and skill. A student might enter a course of study at the elementary or secondary level already knowing enough that he or she will receive an adequate score on the posttest. In other words, the course is likely to duplicate what the student already knows or can do. Possibly that student should be awarded credit and/or enrolled in an advanced course. On the other hand, a student who enters with little information or skill can gain a lot during the course and still be judged inadequate, which is hardly fair. Awarding credit for gain might be a better practice.

- The development of competency in learning—the inductive inquiry skills and the other 21st-century capacities—need to be given major attention. Developing competence in these areas will lead to higher achievement in the subject areas while also building learning capacity. Essentially, learning how to learn is a measureable goal and needs to be recognized as such.

Authors' note: As we begin, we want to recommend that everyone who is inclined to learn how to use formative assessment read the following:

W. James Popham. (2008). *Transformative assessment.* Alexandria, VA: Association for Supervision and Curriculum Development.

We simply cannot do in a short chapter what Popham does in this and several other books. He is sure-footed and *very* knowledgeable. Most of his book is about classroom assessments, formal and informal, in which the results are shared by student and teacher. Popham advocates assessment practices that "lead to instructional adjustment decisions by teachers or learning tactic adjustments by students" (p. 11). His treatment of norm-referenced testing is also outstanding.

MOVING FROM THE SUMMATIVE TRADITION TO THE FORMATIVE ALTERNATIVE

Education bodies have important credentialing functions that have affected assessment traditions. In the earliest grades, teachers are asked to judge whether students are ready for the work of the next grade and whether they need special assistance. As courses become more distinct and teachers more specialized, the core curriculum teachers are asked to make judgments about how well their students have learned mathematics, science, and the other areas. Then the high school is asked to qualify students for a diploma and certify that they have mastered the content of courses needed for admission to higher education. And, today, they are asked to prepare students for tests in Advanced Placement courses, which colleges may elect to accept as fulfilling college course requirements. Educational Testing Service provides these end-of-course, norm-referenced tests.

These evaluation functions have led to the practice of providing "summative" assessments—essentially end-of-course, end-of-year, end-of-school statements about whether learning of the content of the course of study has been adequate or better.

While school faculties cannot just dispense with the responsibility for summative judgments, the summative has overwhelmed the formative, and correction is needed.

PERFORMANCE-ORIENTED AND COMPARISON-ORIENTED MEASURES

Popham (2008) does a wonderful job of distinguishing among the common types of achievement tests and their purposes. Our summary here is parallel to his much longer and very penetrating analysis. Here we distinguish between the following:

- Direct measures of achievement within a course or curriculum that examine *performance*
- Measures designed to compare students on the basis of achievement. Comparisons are most often used to indicate how students in the

class, school, district, or state compare to other students taking the same tests, but they are also commonly used to determine admission to an intervention, institution, or course of study.

Direct Measures of Performance

Direct measures begin with the standards or objectives of the curriculum unit or course of study: what the student is supposed to learn and be able to do. The objectives are laid out, and devices are developed to elicit knowledge or skill. In the case of the curriculum in reading for the primary grades, we set goals such as to be able to read with comprehension books of given levels, to study and unlock new words and passages, and to know at sight (how they are spelled) a body of words. The most direct measures constitute asking the students to read books at various levels, testing comprehension through questions, and asking the students how much they read and how they feel about reading. In addition, they can be presented with a sample of words that they are asked to identify and define.

We can use direct measures in a formative fashion as well as a summative fashion; that is, we can administer them periodically to learn how the students are progressing. We then can share the results with students, parents, and faculty. The information can be used to plan adjustments in instruction for some or all of the students. Formative assessment is a very important part of schoolwide action research. It is very useful as changes are made—as when hybrid courses are developed and need to be tested and modified on the basis of the results. At its heart, direct assessment of performance places the focus on *gains* in knowledge and skill. It also provides an understanding of changes in affect; frequently when a student begins to learn more, the increased capacity is accompanied by a rise in positive feelings about both self and subject.

Assessment needs to be directly based on performance; embedded; continuous; painless; transparent; and used by students, teachers, parents, and policy makers including not only the Responsible Parties but also district and state agencies. Teachers, students, parents, districts, states, and federal government live in a foggy seascape unless we measure gains in knowledge and skill regularly and the data are made transparent to all. Assessment has a major influence on the what, how, and social climate dimensions of the educational environment.

Performance measures can be used to take stock of what has been learned at a summing-up time, such as at the end of the academic year or course; thus the term *summative*. In a sense, summative gains are the basis of the credential. If most of the objectives are achieved to a considerable degree, we can say that the course has been completed. Summative assessment can also indicate when a student has achieved the objectives of courses at a higher level, as when a third grader has achieved the objectives aimed at in the fifth-grade curriculum.

Measuring Gain Is Key

Direct testing of performance related to curriculum standards and objectives can indicate differences between students as individuals and as members of classes, and teachers can learn how well their students achieved the objectives and how much students gained in the process. Measuring gain is the key to all of these uses of assessment. A student who enters with the objectives already mastered cannot gain. A class in which most students enter with considerable prior knowledge can look good on summative measures, but the class did not need to teach much for students to shine on the final tests. On the other hand, students who have poor learning histories have much ground to make up in addition to learning the material in the current course.

The truest measure of student, teacher, instructional materials, and the curriculum itself is how much is learned—what is gained (see Popham, 2008, chap. 7).

When learning is not immediately visible in performance, the instructor can teach in such a way that the student describes internal learning. If a student is trying to comprehend a text passage, the teacher can ask the student to "talk aloud" about the internal process. This tactic raises the student's consciousness of learning as well as providing information to both players in the transaction.

Embedding activities that make learning visible has great merit.

The Response to Intervention framework depends on formative assessment, in which data on gain is central. Determining an initial level of performance starts the formative process. Then the educator collects data frequently to determine both progress being made and the nature of errors that are occurring. Measuring learning formatively informs the educator whether the student or students are responding adequately. If not, then a Tier II modification is begun, and the formative process continues.

The adequacy of learning in the various dimensions of the curriculum areas can be measured against predetermined criteria. Using the example above, fluency in computation, estimation, and knowledge of large cardinal values requires that a high level of mastery be achieved. The facts cannot just be parroted from rote exercises but must be understood. Thus, a very high bar must be set—100 percent correct when a brief time to respond is allowed. Teachers who share writing scales that describe the dimensions of writing quality in a genre and a variety of sample papers that are rated highly are using the writing scales and the sample papers to show students the criteria of excellent performance. If, at the beginning of a course of study, the teacher has students write to a prompt and assesses student responses analytically in relation to the shared criteria, she is using criterion-referenced assessment. If she does something similar at the end of the course, she can look at gain in writing quality in that genre.

If the teacher wants to move into formative assessment, there are a variety of directions she can take. Here's one. At the beginning of the course, after she has rated and returned the initial samples of writing, she asks students to compare their work to the criteria and leads discussions in which students come to see the criteria as goals for the course. The students raise questions when they have difficulty applying the criteria to their own writing.

Using the student results she entered into the Excel spreadsheet, her notes on errors, and her discussions with students, the teacher designs instruction to move the students forward as writers. She also asks students to identify specific aspects of their writing they wish to improve and list at least three things they can do to get started. She will have them practice writing short pieces, in only 10 or 15 minutes, 2 or 3 times a week so she can see how effective her instruction is and if common errors are disappearing and the presentation of ideas is improving. Students will also be assessing their progress on the goals and actions they identified.

It may be four weeks or six weeks before the teacher gives the students another formal assessment. During the time she is working with these students, they will have three to six formal assessments as well as many informal assessments, which both teacher and student will use to shape instruction and personal actions. This teacher and her students are using criterion-referenced assessment and formative assessment, and they can all measure gain. At the end of the course of study, they also have summative data.

The development of benchmarks related to curriculum standards requires the establishment of criteria for performance, that is, when performance is adequate at a basic level and when it is better than basic or at a high level of performance. The National Assessment of Educational Progress (NAEP) is developing criteria in many areas. For an example, you might examine the expectations of student performance across a variety of text types at Grades 4, 8, and 12. (The Reading Achievement-Level Descriptions are available in the various documents at http://nces.ed.gov/nationsreportcard/reading/achieveall.asp.) Of course, the NAEP is not for formative assessment of or for learning.

Normative, Comparison-Oriented Measures

Most of the "standardized" tests used by national, state, and local educational agencies are of the normative stripe. Rather than being thorough assessments of the major standards and objectives of the curriculum areas, these tests sample items related to those standards and objectives. As items are built and piloted, test makers eliminate items answered correctly by a large proportion of the students! Now, why would they do that, when those items indicate that the relevant curricular objective has been achieved? They do so because items answered correctly (or incorrectly) by a majority of the students do not discriminate between students. They want to include items answered correctly by between 40 and 60 percent of the students. They build a test on which the *average* students answer about half of the items correctly. They prefer to report results in percentiles or standard scores (ranks based on standard deviations).

Such tests have little diagnostic value because they are not keyed to the curriculum objectives being taught. And, since the test makers are surveying a wide range of knowledge in a limited time frame, often an hour for a subject area, the tests may contain very few items related to a given major objective. If the objective involves skill in solving a given type of equation, the test can give the students only two or three tries. Or, if there are 50 facts (such as multiplication "facts"), again only 2 or 3 are included in the test. Getting true diagnostic information would require testing all of the facts so that the faculty could learn which ones need more (or less) attention.

To summarize, our priorities with respect to assessment are the following:

- To shift assessment priorities from the summative to the formative
- To measure performance directly rather than indirectly and normatively

How much change does the implementation of gain-oriented performance assessment represent? The answer is that a very large change has to be generated, one that involves a considerable revision in tradition. The concept of assessing performance has been around for a long time, and tools for doing it abound. Tradition has held back progress. This tradition is reinforced by the very powerful publishers of tests and by the previous and current federal government administrations, and it is massively supported by the officials responsible for the administration of No Child Left Behind.

SHARING EVALUATION DATA: AUDIENCES

Who should be the recipients of assessment data? We could just say, "Everybody," but communication of formative assessment, while it overlaps for different audiences, is also different for different audiences. Clearly the following audiences are important:

- **Teachers and learners:** Regular measurement of progress is essential so that teachers and learners have a healthy picture of progress. And some assessment information becomes a part of their interaction. As teachers provide learning tasks or teachers and students decide on them, both can easily figure out whether they can accomplish them and how they will see evidence of learning. In addition, regular semiformal or formal collection of data enables them to chart progress. The information can also be shared with parents. Accumulating data for the year gives a summative picture of gain; a separate "summative" measure should not be needed.

- **Faculties and Responsible Parties:** Collecting data from the classes or organizational units provides a picture of progress throughout the school. In addition, educators and school leaders need to select schoolwide assessments in important areas and work together to collect and organize data as a part of their action research process. For example, they may learn to use a common measure of quality of writing and use it to measure gain in all classes at intervals. Using measures across grade levels can provide a picture of progress throughout the period of student enrollment, such as K–8, 9–12, and other combinations. As at the school level, accumulating data throughout the year gives a year-end, summative picture.

- **School district policy makers:** For this audience, measuring student learning (gain) across the curriculum areas and in all schools is an essential goal. As initiatives are designed to improve learning, their effects can be calculated. On the whole, evaluations of initiatives need to draw on the base data. For example, districtwide Tier II RTI programs need to be assessed in terms of whether they generate gains for the students involved. Usually school-level data, accumulated for the district, are sufficient, and an additional districtwide measurement program is not needed.

- **State and national policy makers:** The process at state and national levels is similar to that at the district level except that data management is more complex. If schools and districts are conducting good formative studies in the core curriculum areas, no large-scale state or national testing programs should be needed.

In sum, the results should be transparent to all concerned.

13 An Optimistic Future

I wouldn't claim that we know enough to have "fail-safe" routes to innovation. But there is a well-documented base of research, evaluation, and experience to guide us and help us avoid some of the perennial sinkholes. The well-informed will succeed, using their imaginations and problem-solving ability to fill in the gaps.

. . . Our Reflective Observer

We see ourselves as realistic optimists. We have been part of some good efforts that have made some big differences to a lot of students and have confidence that school improvement efforts can be designed to make significant differences to practice and student learning. But the overall national picture is worrisome. We are aggravated by the evidence (as from the National Assessment of Educational Progress [NAEP], http://nces.ed.gov/nationsreportcard/) that U.S. academic achievement has remained relatively flat despite some huge and expensive efforts by our national government. We have some really outstanding schools, including a good number that serve all types of populations and are not intimidated by diversity. There are important lessons from the frustrations of failure and the celebrations of the best.

High-quality implementation of ICT will depend almost entirely on the teaching/learning strategies that are employed. Also, we need to remember that not all offerings that are ICT based or that incorporate the Internet will be of high quality. Bad online courses can be deadly to learning, and replacing campus courses with all but the best distance-learning options can *reduce* educational efficiency. However, we have seen some stunning examples of high-quality development, including from teachers we know.

> ### A Final Thought on Change
>
> One reason that our educational system is slow to change comes from its role as a stabilizer. Transmitting the culture is a conserving business. Schooling was developed to send culture along to the next generation without modifying it greatly. Any kind of change will be greeted with murmurs of worry and clucking noises.
>
> When the computer first appeared, courses on "keyboarding" appeared quickly; these were akin to previous generations' touch-typing courses. Courses on how to use computers to enhance quality of expression were rare, however. When the World Wide Web burst onto the scene, the main initial response by schools was not to help students exploit the new resources but rather to build firewalls so that the children would not be led astray by digital pornography and such.
>
> These responses are completely understandable, if extreme at times.
>
> Nonetheless, the introduction of digital media and the connection of the home and school platforms will destabilize many aspects of schooling.

CODA: BIG CLAIMS, WORRIES ABOUT OUR BRAINS, AND SOLID PROGRESS—FROM OMG TO HARD WORK

As digital tools continue to proliferate and ICT becomes more present in schools and homes, we are bound to have a spate of books celebrating it, worrying about it, and providing advice about direction to take to make it pay off for education. Curtis Bonk's 2009 book fits the first category. The subtitle, *How Web Technology Is Revolutionizing Education*, captures its aspirations and its weaknesses. The book is a pastiche of real and possible applications, but we are a long way from the "is revolutionizing" claim. The subtitle is the flipside of Wagner's 2008 *Why Even Our Best Schools Don't Teach the Survival Skills Our Children Need—and What We Can Do About It*, which has a bit of OMG hyperbole.

Capitalizing on the media attention given to his 2008 *Atlantic* article, "Is Google Making Us Stupid," Nicholas Carr's interesting 2010 book, *The Shallows*, deals with conceptions of the neurological system, particularly its "plasticity." The publisher calls *Shallows* an "explosive book on technology's effect on the mind." OMG again. As Anthony Cocciolo points out in his 2010 review in the *Teachers College Record*, Carr writes with a "declarative" tone and a "technological determinist" frame of reference, neither borne out by his argument or conceptual organization.

However, Carr's work provides a useful function by underlining changing conceptions of the neurological system, particularly the brain, from the perspective of *plasticity*. For many years, psychologists and biologists believed that the brain was a relatively fixed set of programmed cells whose functions were determined by genetics and, perhaps, by early socialization into a culture and its subset, the family. The result was a machine that carried out the jobs it had been trained to do. Now, the brain is thought to be far more adaptive—hence the term *plasticity*—responding to the demands of its environment by developing new programs. New habits result.

This somewhat plastic organ can reinvent itself across cultures and eras.

Grow up in America and, lo! American circuits appear. Move to France, and some Frenchness is grafted on to the American circuits. Grow up in a culture without print literacy, and you will learn to remember things from being told them or observing them. Grow up in a culture with print literacy, and you will not develop as much capacity to remember things by being told them, but you will learn to process text in print (see Ong, 2002). Grow up with the telephone, and you will learn to listen and speak without observing the person with whom you communicate. Grow up before radio and the gramophone, and constant entertainment will not fill your neurological world.

And so on.

The media technologies of various eras have a huge impact, and adaptation or lack of it greatly affects one's interaction with the people of one's time. Expertness in print literacy has been a key to success and pleasure for the last 300 years in European society. Poor literacy skills have made success difficult and deprived one of a major source of pleasure and information.

There are upsides and downsides to each adaptation.

Everyone who reads these pages knows the upside of literacy. However, we also know that people can escape into reading—they can lose themselves in unreal worlds while their lives slip away. The passageways of the brain became a habituated avenue in which they became lost.

Recorded music has brought great pleasure. But since it came about, fewer people have learned the skills of playing the piano and singing around it, and what was once a commonplace tool is now regarded as one that is difficult to master. A massive library of recordings promises endless listening. It also fosters the habit of turning on music when starting the car or before opening the cookbook or reaching for any book at all. The habituated practices of adaptation to one medium can affect the tenor of life. We can lose the "sounds of silence, our old friend."

Carr (2010) worries that our adaptation to immersion in media is changing our brains in ways we will regret. Can texting, tweeting, facebooking, Googling, etc. create a nerve-wracking, jumpy environment to which our brains are adapting—with the loss of calm, thoughtful pursuits? Or, in Maureen Dowd's (2010) words, is technology a narcotic? Will virtual schools create an isolated, almost antisocial place, but one in which our brains have learned to live? A frantic place—but one our minds call home.

The pace of change requires that we find avenues to capitalize on the potential of technology. Ensuring that it remains a tool and not our master will require serious reflection and action. The mind is more powerful than the media, but we know it is possible to work at less than our potential or just engage in patterned behavior while carelessly pushing away our reflective powers.

Carr (2010) refers repeatedly to the possibility of losing the capacity for "deep reading." We are reminded that policies that have nothing to do with ICT can affect what we are given to read. Several of the prominent professional organizations are restricting the length of the articles in their magazines because "educators are too busy to read long pieces." Several journals now want no articles longer than 300 words. Wow! That will make sure that there is nothing to read deeply. And these are educators making that policy?

We have much to learn.

What Now?

We need to get down to the business of using ICT to build better courses for all students and make another mighty attempt to build equal opportunity through education. The World Wide Web brings the New Library to our schools and to families at the kitchen table.

We will use the emerging technological gifts cheerfully to extend our capabilities and the learning capacity of our students. And, as new tools come over the horizon, we will find that we need to change again and again. It is a great time to be alive.

References

Agee, J., & Altarriba, J. (2009). Changing conceptions and uses of computer technologies in the everyday: Literacy practices of sixth and seventh graders. *Research in the Teaching of English, 43*(4), 363–396.

Aiken, W. (1942). *The story of the eight-year study: With conclusions and recommendations.* New York: Harper.

Allen, L., & Calhoun, E. F. (1998). Schoolwide action research: Findings from six years of study. *Phi Delta Kappan, 79*(9), 706–710.

Allington, R. L., & McGill-Franzen, A. (2003). The impact of summer reading setback on the reading achievement gap. *Phi Delta Kappan, 85*(1), 68–75.

Almy, M. (1970). *Logical thinking in second grade.* New York, NY: Teachers College Press.

Atwood, M., & Weaver, R. (Eds.). (1995). *New Oxford book of Canadian short stories in English.* Toronto, Canada: Oxford University Press.

Avenues. (n.d.). About Avenues, the World School. Available at http://www.avenues.org/world-school/

Bailey, A. L., & Heritage, M. (2008). *Formative assessment for literacy, Grades K–6: Building reading and academic language skills across the curriculum.* Thousand Oaks, CA: Corwin.

Ball, S., & Bogatz, G. A. (1970). *The first year of* Sesame Street*: An evaluation.* Princeton, NJ: Educational Testing Service.

Barr, R., Kamil, M. L., Mosenthal, P., & Pearson, P. D. (1996). *Handbook of reading research: Vol. II.* Mahwah, NJ: Lawrence Erlbaum Associates. (Originally published 1991)

Bennett, L., & Berson, M. J. (Eds.). (2007). *Digital age: Technology-based K–12 lesson plans for social studies.* Silver Spring, MD: National Council for the Social Studies.

Bernard, R. M., Abrami, P. C., Lou, Y., Borokhovski, E., Wade, A., Wozney, L., . . . Huang, B. (2004). How does distance education compare to classroom instruction? A meta-analysis of the empirical literature. *Review of Educational Research, 74*(3), 379–439.

Blankinship, D. G. (2010, June 27). School libraries fading as budget crisis deepens. Associated Press in the *Washington Times.* Available at http://www.washingtontimes.com/news/2010/jun/27/school-libraries-fading-as-budget-crisis-deepens/

Blase, J., & Blase, J. (2000). *Empowering teachers: What successful principals do* (2nd ed.). Thousand Oaks, CA: Corwin.

Blecksmith, A. Visual resources online: Digital images of primary materials on public Web sites. *C&RL News, (69)*, 5, 275–278. (Also available at http://crln .acrl.org/content/69/5/275.full.pdf)

Bloom, B. S., Hastings, T., & Madaus, G. (1971). *Handbook of formative and summative evaluation of student learning*. New York: McGraw-Hill.

Bonk, C. J. (2009). *The world is open: How web technology is revolutionizing education.* San Francisco, CA: Jossey-Bass.

Bonsangue, M. V. (1993). Long-term effects of the calculus workshop model. *Cooperative Learning, 13*(3), 19–20.

Bredderman, T. A. (1973). The effects of training on the ability to control variables. *Journal of Research in Science Teaching, 10*, 189–200.

Bredderman, T. A. (1983). Effects of activity-based elementary science on student outcomes: A quantitative analysis. *Review of Educational Research, 53*, 499–518.

Buehl, D. (2001). *Classroom strategies for interactive learning* (2nd ed.). Newark, DE: International Reading Association. (There is also a third edition, 2009, of this excellent resource.)

Calhoun, E. F. (1994). *How to use action research in the self-renewing school.* Alexandria, VA: Association for Supervision and Curriculum Development.

Calhoun, E. F. (1997). *Literacy for all.* Saint Simons Island, GA: Phoenix Alliance.

Calhoun, E. F. (1999). *Teaching beginning reading and writing with the Picture Word Inductive Model.* Alexandria, VA: Association for Supervision and Curriculum Development.

Calhoun, E. F. (2002). Action research for school improvement. *Educational Leadership, 59*(6), 18–24.

Calhoun, E. F. (2004). *Using data to assess your reading program.* Alexandria, VA: Association for Supervision and Curriculum Development.

Carr, N. (2008). Is Google making us stupid? *Atlantic*, July/August. Retrieved from http://www.theatlantic.com/magazine/archive/2008/07/is-google-making-us-stupid/6868/

Carr, N. (2010). *The shallows: What the Internet is doing to our brains.* New York, NY: W. W. Norton.

CCSSO (Council of Chief State School Officers). (2011). *Interstate Teacher Assessment and Support Consortium (InTASC) Model Core Teaching Standards: A resource for state dialogue.* Washington, DC: Author. Available at http://www.ccsso.org/intasc/

Clardy, A. (2009). *Distant, on-line education: Effects, principles, and practices.* Online submission to Education Resources Information Center. Available from ERIC database (ED506182)

Cocciolo, A. (2010). [Review of the book *The Shallows: What the Internet Is Doing to Our Brains* by Nicholas Carr]. *Teachers College Record*, November 11.

Common Core. (2009). *Why we're behind: What top nations teach their students but we don't.* Washington, DC: Author. Retrieved from http://www.commoncore .org/_docs/CCreport_whybehind.pdf

Coughlin, E. (2010). High school at a crossroads. *Educational Leadership, 67*(7), 48–53. Retrieved from http://learningthenow.com/blog/wp-content/uploads/2010/05/High-Schools-at-a-Crossroads-Ed-Coughlin2.pdf

Counts, G. S. (1978). *Dare the school build a new social order?* Carbondale: Southern Illinois University Press. (Originally published 1932)

Cunningham, P. M. (1990). The Names Test: A quick assessment of decoding ability. *The Reading Teacher, 44*, 124–199.

Cunningham, P. M. (2005). *Phonics they use: Words for reading and writing* (4th ed.). Boston, MA: Pearson-Allyn & Bacon.

Deshler, D. D., Palincsar, A. S., Biancarosa, G., & Nair, M. (2007). *Informed choices for struggling adolescent readers*. Newark, DE: International Readng Association.

Dillon, S. (2010, February 12). Wi-Fi turns rowdy bus into rolling study hall. *New York Times*. Retrieved from http://www.nytimes.com/2010/02/12/education/12bus.html

Dowd, M. (2010, June 27). Are cells the new cigarettes? *New York Times*. Retrieved from http://www.nytimes.com/2010/06/27/opinion/27dowd.html

El-Nemr, M. A. (1979). Meta-analysis of the outcomes of teaching biology as inquiry. Doctoral dissertation, University of Colorado at Boulder, CO.

Federal Communications Commission. (n.d.). *National broadband plan: Connecting America*. Retrieved from http://www.broadband.gov/plan/

Foderaro, L. W. (2010). For college students, it's paper over pixels. *International Herald Tribune*, October 21, p. 16.

Gabel, D. (Ed.). (1994). *Handbook of research on science teaching and learning*. New York, NY: Macmillan.

Gersten, R., Fuchs, L. S., Williams, J. P., & Baker, S. (2001). Teaching reading comprehension strategies to students with learning disabilities: A review of research. *Review of Educational Research, 71*(2), 279–320. doi:10.3102/00346543071002279

Glickman, C. D. (1993). *Renewing America's schools: A guide for school-based action*. San Francisco, CA: Jossey-Bass.

Graham, S. (2009–2010). Want to improve children's writing? Don't neglect their handwriting. *American Educator, 33*(4), 20–27, 40. Retrieved from http://www.aft.org/pdfs/americaneducator/winter2009/graham.pdf

Graham, S., Harris, K. R., & Fink, B. (2000). Is handwriting causally related to learning to write? Treatment of handwriting problems in beginning writers. *Journal of Educational Psychology, 92*(4), 620–633. doi:10.1037/0022-0663.92.4.620

Graham, S., & Weintraub, N. (1996). A review of handwriting research: Progress and prospects from 1980 to 1994. *Education Psychology Review, 8*(1), 7–87. doi:10.1007/BF01761831

Hampton, S., & Resnick, L. B. (2009). *Reading and writing with understanding: Comprehension in fourth and fifth grades*. Newark, DE: International Reading Association.

Harkreader, S., & Weathersby, J. (1998). *Staff development and student achievement: Making the connection in Georgia schools*. Atlanta: Georgia State University, Council for School Performance.

Harvey, O. J., Hunt, D. E., & Schroder, H. M. (1961). *Conceptual systems and personality organization*. New York: John Wiley & Sons.

Hill, P., & Johnston, M. (2010). In the future, diverse approaches to schooling. *Phi Delta Kappan, 92*(3), 43–47. Retrieved from http://www.kappanmagazine.org/site/misc/Kappan92_MustReads2.pdf, 22–30.

Hillocks, G. (1987). Synthesis of research on teaching writing. *Educational Leadership, 44*(8), 71–82.

Hord, S. M. (1997). *Professional learning communities: Communities of continuous inquiry and improvement*. Austin, TX: Southwest Educational Development Laboratory. Retrieved from http://www.sedl.org/pubs/catalog/items/cha34.html

Hord, S. M., Roussin, J. L., & Sommers, W. A. (2009). *Guiding professional learning communities: Inspiration, challenge, surprise, and meaning*. Thousand Oaks, CA: Corwin.

Hord, S. M., & Sommers, W. A. (2007). *Leading professional learning communities: Voices from research and practice.* Thousand Oaks, CA: Corwin.

Hunt, D. E., & Sullivan, E. V. (1974). *Between psychology and education.* Hinsdale, IL: Dryden Press.

IASCE (International Association for the Study of Cooperation in Education). (2011, February). *Newsletter, 30*(1).

Iowa Association of School Boards. (2007). *Leadership for student learning.* Des Moines, IA: Author.

Johnson, D. W., & Johnson, R. T. (1999). *Learning together and alone: Cooperative, competitive, and individualistic learning* (5th ed.). Boston, MA: Allyn & Bacon.

Joyce, B. R. (1972a). *The magic lantern: Metaphor for humanistic education.* Paper presented at the Annual Meeting of the American Education Research Association, Chicago, April. Available from ERIC database (ED065466)

Joyce, B. R. (1972b). *The teacher and his staff: Man, media, and machines.* Washington, DC: National Commission on Teacher Education and Professional Standards and Center for the Study of Instruction, National Education Association of the United States.

Joyce, B. R., & Calhoun, E. F. (Eds.). (1996). *Learning experiences in school renewal: An exploration of five successful programs.* Eugene, OR: ERIC Clearinghouse on Educational Management. Available from ERIC database (ED401600)

Joyce, B. R., & Calhoun, E. F. (1998). *Learning to teach inductively.* Boston, MA: Allyn & Bacon.

Joyce, B. R., & Calhoun, E. F. (2010). *Models of professional development: A celebration of educators.* Thousand Oaks, CA: Corwin.

Joyce, B. R., Calhoun, E. F., Jutras, J., & Newlove, K. (2006). *Scaling up: The results of a literacy curriculum implemented in an entire education authority of 53 schools.* Paper presented at the Asian Pacific Educational Research Association, Hong Kong.

Joyce, B. R., & Clift, R. (1984). The phoenix agenda: Essential reform in teacher education. *Educational Researcher 13*(4), 5–18.

Joyce, B. R., Peck, L., & Brown, C. (1981). *Flexibility in teaching.* New York: Longman.

Joyce, B. R., & Showers, B. (2002). *Student achievement through staff development* (3rd ed.). Alexandria, VA: Association for Supervision and Curriculum Development.

Joyce, B. R., Weil, M., & Calhoun, E. F. (2009). *Models of teaching* (8th ed.). Boston, MA: Pearson/Allyn & Bacon.

Kellman, P., Massey, C., Roth, Z., Burke, T., Zucker, J., Saw, A., Aguero, K., & Wise, J. (2008). Perceptual learning and the technology of expertise. *Pragmatics & Cognition, 16*(2), 356–405.

Leithwood, K., & Jantzi, D. (2009). A review of empirical evidence about school size effects: A policy perspective. *Review of Educational Research, 79,* 464–490.

Lewin, T. (2010, January 20). Children awake? Then they're probably online. *New York Times.* Retrieved from http://www.nytimes.com/2010/01/20/education/20wired.html

Loucks-Horsley, S. (2003). *Designing professional development for teachers of science and mathematics.* Thousand Oaks, CA: Corwin.

McGill-Franzen, A., Allington, R. L., Yokoi, L., & Brooks, G. (1999). Putting books in the room seems necessary but not sufficient. *Journal of Educational Research, 93*(2), 67–74.

McKinsey & Company. (2007). *How the world's best-performing school systems come out on top.* New York, NY: Author. Retrieved from http://www.mckinsey .com/App_Media/Reports/SSO/Worlds_School_Systems_Final.pdf

Mourshed, M., Chijioke, C., & Barber, M. (2010). *How the world's most improved school systems keep getting better.* New York, NY: McKinsey. Retrieved from http://ssomckinsey.darbyfilms.com/reports/EducationBookNov23.pdf

NAEP (National Assessment of Educational Progress). (2007). *The Condition of Education 2007.* Washington, DC: National Center for Education Statistics. Available at http://nces.ed.gov/programs/coe/

NAEP (National Assessment of Educational Progress). (2010). *The Condition of Education 2010.* Washington, DC: National Center for Education Statistics. Available at http://nces.ed.gov/programs/coe/

NCES (National Center for Educational Statistics). (2010). *The nation's report card: Reading 2009.* Retrieved from http://nces.ed.gov/nationsreportcard/pdf/main2009/2010458.pdf

OECD (Organisation for Economic Co-operation and Development Programme). (2007). *PISA 2006: Science competencies for tomorrow's world.* OECD briefing note for the United States. Retrieved from http://www.oecd.org/dataoecd/16/28/39722597.pdf

OECD (Organisation for Economic Co-operation and Development Programme). (2010). *PISA 2009 results: What students know and can do—Student performance in reading, mathematics, and science: Vol I.* Paris: Author. http://dx.doi.org/10.1787/9789264091450-en

OECD (Organisation for Economic Co-operation and Development Programme). (2011). *Strong Performers and successful reformers in education: Lessons from PISA for the United States.* Paris: Author. http://dx.doi.org/10.1787/9789264096660-en

OECD (Organisation for Economic Co-operation and Development Programme for International Student Assessment). (2007). *PISA 2006: Science competencies for tomorrow's world: Volume 1-Analysis.* Paris: Author. (Full text available online: http://www.oecd.org/dataoecd/30/17/39703267.pdf.)

Ong, W. J. (2002). *Orality and literacy: The technologizing of the word.* New York, NY: Routledge.

Ortega y Gasset, J. (1992). *Mission of the university.* New Brunswick, NJ: Transaction. (Originally published 1930)

P21, SETDA, & ISTE (Partnership for 21st Century Skills, State Educational Technology Directors Association, & International Society for Technology in Education). (2007). *Maximizing the impact: The pivotal role of technology in a 21st century education system.* Retrieved from http://www.p21.org/documents/p21setdaistepaper.pdf

Pasnik, S., Bates, L., Brunner, C., Cervantes, F., Hupert, N., Schindel, J., & Townsend, E. (2010). *Ready to learn summative evaluation.* New York, NY: Center for Children and Technology.

Pinnell, G. S., Lyons C. A., Deford, D. E., Bryk, A., & Seltzer, M. (1994). Comparing instructional models for the literacy education of high-risk first graders. *Reading Research Quarterly, 29,* 8–39.

Popham, W. J. (2008). *Transformative assessment.* Alexandria, VA: Association for Supervision and Curriculum Development.

Prensky, M. (2010). *Teaching digital natives: Partnering for real learning.* Thousand Oaks, CA: Corwin.

Resnick, L. B., Hampton, S., & the New Standards Primary Literacy Committee. (2009). *Reading and writing: Grade by grade* (Rev. ed.). Newark, DE: International Reading Association.

Riel, M., & Fulton, K. (2001). The role of technology in supporting learning communities. *Phi Delta Kappan, 82*(7), 518–526.

Rosenthal, E. (2010, May 29). Our fix-it faith and the oil spill. *New York Times.* Retrieved from http://www.nytimes.com/2010/05/30/weekinreview/30rosenthal.html

Schwab, J. J. (1965). *Biological Sciences Curriculum Study: Biology teachers' handbook.* New York, NY: John Wiley and Sons.

Schwartz, R. M. (2005). Literacy learning of at-risk first-grade students in the Reading Recovery intervention. *Journal of Educational Psychology, 97*(2), 257–267.

Schwartz, R. M., & Raphael, T. E. (1985). Concept of definition: A key to improving students' vocabulary. *The Reading Teacher, 39*(2), 198–205.

Sharan, S., & Shachar, H. (1988). *Language and learning in the cooperative classroom.* New York, NY: Springer-Verlag.

Singularity University. (2011). "History & founding." http://singularityu.org/about/history/.

Slavin, R. E. (1983). *Cooperative learning.* New York, NY: Longman.

Slavin, R. E. (1994). *Cooperative learning: Theory, research, and practice* (2nd ed.). Boston, MA: Allyn & Bacon.

Slavin, R. E., Madden, N. A., Chambers, B., & Haxby, B. (2009). *2 million children: Success for all.* Thousand Oaks, CA: Corwin.

Smith, D. (2008). *The Penguin state of the world atlas* (8th ed.). New York, NY: Penguin Books.

Stross, R. (2011, February 5). Online courses, still lacking that third dimension. *New York Times.* Retrieved from http://www.nytimes.com/2011/02/06/business/06digi.html

Taub, E. A. (2010, February 27). The web way to learn a language. *New York Times.* Retrieved from http://www.nytimes.com/2010/01/28/technology/personaltech/28basics.html

Tucker, M. S. (2011). *Standing on the shoulders of giants: An American agenda for education reform.* Washington, DC: National Center on Education and the Economy (NCEE). Retrieved from http://www.ncee.org./wp-content/uploads/2011/05/Standing-on-the-Shoulders-of-Giants-An-American-Agenda-for-Education-Reform.pdf

U.S. Department of Education, Office of Educational Technology. (2010). *Transforming American education: Learning powered by technology.* Retrieved from http://www.ed.gov/sites/default/files/NETP-2010-final-report.pdf

Vance, A. (2010, June 13). Merely human? That's so yesterday. *New York Times.* Retrieved from http://www.nytimes.com/2010/06/13/business/13sing.html

Wagner, T. (2008). *The global achievement gap: Why even our best schools don't teach the new survival skills our children need—and what we can do about it.* New York: Basic Books.

Wiederholt, J. L., & Bryant, B. R. (2001). *Gray Oral Reading Tests* (4th ed.). Austin, TX: Pro-Ed.

Zhao, Y., Lei, J., Yan, B., Lai, C., & Tan, H. S. (2005). What makes the difference? A practical analysis of research on the effectiveness of distance education. *Teachers College Record, 107*(8), 1836–1884. Retrieved from http://ott.educ.msu.edu/literature/report.pdf

INTERNET RESOURCES CITED IN LESSON EXAMPLES OR SCENARIOS

America's Dairy Farmers: http://www.dairyfarmingtoday.org/

David Warlick's Landmarks for Schools: http://landmark-project.com/ (a number of useful links for social studies, science, and the application of mathematics)

Emigration/Immigration: http://maggieblanck.com/Immigration.html (photographs and commentary, developed by Maggie Blanck in the course of an inquiry into her family's history)

Google Earth: http://earth.google.com/

International Business Etiquette and Manners: http://www.cyborlink.com/besite/ (etiquette in other countries)

Kidblog.org: http://kidblog.org/ (blog setup)

Library of Congress country profiles: http://lcweb2.loc.gov/frd/cs/profiles.html

Library of Congress: http://loc.gov/index.html

Merriam-Webster: http://www.m-w.com/ (free online dictionary that includes audio pronunciations)

National Library of Virtual Mathematics from Utah State University: http://nvlm.usu/en/nav/vlibrary.html

National Science Teachers Association Learning Center: http://learningcenter.nsta.org/ (NSTA's "e-professional development portal")

Teacher's Discovery: http://www.teachersdiscovery.com/

TumbleBooks: http://www.tumblebooks.com/

United Nations: http://cyberschoolbus.un.org/

Wikipedia: http://en.wikipedia.org/

Zoho Show: https://show.zoho.com/ (presentation tool)

Annotated Bibliography

I. THEMES

We have been inspired by the surviving writings of the philosophers from the Greek classics to *The Audacity of Hope*. We'll list just a couple here. Ortega y Gasset captured the essence of modern education in a succinct and compelling style. Halberstam dealt with our culture incisively, captured the changes that electronic media were making in our behavior and, in so doing, forecast our current promises.

Halberstam, D. (1993). *The fifties.* New York, NY: Random House.

Ortega y Gasset, J. (1992). *Mission of the university.* New Brunswick, NJ: Transaction. (Original work published 1930).

II. PROBLEMS TO ADDRESS

Needs are everywhere, but the secondary school is falling apart. Coughlin captured one of the current dilemmas eloquently. Kirn brought forward a major problem that is usually swept under the pundit rug.

Calderón, M. (2007). *Teaching reading to English language learners, Grades 6–12: A framework for improving achievement in the content areas.* Thousand Oaks, CA: Corwin.

> Deals with one of the major issues in American education. Millions of students need to be helped—again, *right now*!

Coughlin, E. (2010). High school at a crossroads. *Educational Leadership, 67*(7), 48–53. Retrieved from http://learningthenow.com/blog/wp-content/uploads/2010/05/High-Schools-at-a-Crossroads-Ed-Coughlin2.pdf

> Coughlin presents the disturbing proposition that many high schools may become mere credential-counting offices as students present credits rather

than attending on-campus courses. As some districts build virtual high schools, they are inviting that consequence.

Joyce, B. R., & Clift, R. (1984). The phoenix agenda: Essential reform in teacher education. *Educational Researcher,13*(4), 5–18. doi:10.3102/0013189X013004005

After all these years, the issues facing teacher education have not changed much. In a worst-case scenario, the much-maligned teacher education curriculum may simply go online.

Kirn, W. (2010, February 28). Class dismissed. *New York Times Magazine*, 11–12. Retrieved at http://www.nytimes.com/2010/02/28/magazine/28FOB-wwln-t.html

After describing the weird changes in the senior year for many students, Kirn raises a reasonable question. Essentially, the year represents a chunk of life that should have a fine and academic quality. If we can't provide that, he argues, perhaps we'd be better off eliminating it.

Krugman, P. (2011, March 6). Degrees and dollars. *New York Times*, p. A19. Retrieved from http://www.nytimes.com/2011/03/07/opinion/07krugman.html

Points out that education as we have known it will not solve the problems of unemployment because technology is taking the place of many operations that were previously done by people—a very serious challenge.

Rao, K., Eady, M., & Edelen-Smith, P. (2011). Creating virtual classrooms for rural and remote communities. *Phi Delta Kappan, 92*(6), 22–27.

This is an obvious application of ICT. Essentially states, and possibly the nation, should become hot spots. Rural teachers can develop fabulous hybrid courses that take the world to their students.

Scherer, M. (2011). Transforming education with technology: A conversation with Karen Cator. *Educational Leadership, 68*(5), 16–21.

Cator is the director of the Office of Educational Technology in the U.S. Department of Education. Cator is down to earth. She agrees with our contention that teachers are not immigrants to a new country inhabited by more technology-efficient students. "We have to get beyond calling teachers digital immigrants" (p. 21). On the other hand, she stresses that we are just at the beginning stages of capitalizing on ICT.

III. PROVOCATIVE ANALYSES: A SAMPLING

Ash, K. (2009). Maine 1-to-1 effort moves forward. *Education Week Digital Directions*, 3(1), 14–15. Retrieved from http://www.edweek.org/dd/articles/2009/10/21/01maine.h03.html

Maine's effort to try to put computers into the hands of *every* student is worth applauding.

Bonk, C. J. (2009). *The world is open: How web technology is revolutionizing education.* San Francisco, CA: Jossey-Bass.

The futurists are concentrating on artificial intelligence, first augmenting human intelligence and then, possibly, surpassing it.

Brooks, D. (2010, July 8). The medium is the medium. *New York Times*, p. A17. Retrieved from http://www.nytimes.com/2010/07/09/opinion/09brooks.html

The always-thoughtful Brooks comments on how what becomes captured by a media presentation becomes a reality in its own right.

Carr, N. (2010). *The shallows: What the Internet is doing to our brains.* New York, NY: W. W. Norton.

An omigod analysis. Claims that our minds are being "Googled."

Collins, A., & Halverson, R. (2009). *Rethinking education in the age of technology: The digital revolution and schooling in America.* New York, NY: Teachers College Press.

A general treatment of many ICT possibilities.

Dalton School. (2010). The Dalton Technology Plan. Retrieved from http://dalton .org/program/technology/plan/

A small private school, long a star, is not afraid to move into the new world.

Hess, F. M., & Meeks, O. M. (2010). Unbundling schools. *Phi Delta Kappan, 92*(3), 41–42.

Some conservative educators really outdo themselves in their desire to control the curriculum through virtual schools.

Ong, W. (2002). *Orality and literacy: The technologizing of the word.* London, UK: Routledge.

This seminal piece raises the issue of whether long centuries of changing practice affect cognitions.

The Open University (http://www.open.ac.uk/)

Founded 50 years ago by the government, The Open University offers not only a full undergraduate menu but a great number of graduate programs. From the beginning it has used distance means (broadcast television has only recently been discontinued because other technologies now fill its place) supplemented with tutorial centers. Evaluation of courses is rigorous. Many students are employed full-time (most employers have helped out with time and money) and more than 3,000,000 have graduated. As ICT becomes more accessible and its resources richer, OU will only get better. We have a special fondness because we have had extensive contact with their press, including publishing with them, and have become acquainted with their enthusiastic and very competent staff.

Prensky, M. (2010). *Teaching digital natives: Partnering for real learning.* Thousand Oaks, CA: Corwin.

The title has captured the imaginations of many people, but it is a somewhat romantic depiction of young folks and a pessimistic view of older folks, such as teachers. The idea that the school can become out-of-date with respect to the mainstream culture is a serious one.

Vance, A. (2010, June 13). Merely human? That's so yesterday. *New York Times*, pp. BU1–BU2. Retrieved from http://www.nytimes.com/2010/06/13/business/13sing.html

Discusses the Singularity movement with its emphasis on using very complex advances to support and enhance human capacity.

Promises Fulfilled by Distance Media for Half a Century

Two marvelous initiatives capture the immensity of social change that can be generated by distance education: The Open University and *Sesame Street*. Here are two studies, 40 years apart, that came to the same positive conclusion about *Sesame Street*.

Ball, S., & Bogatz, G. A. (1970). *The first year of* Sesame Street. Princeton, NJ: Educational Testing Service.

An early and very thorough study. Effects on language development were greatest where schools as well as homes brought the program to the children and teachers were active in following up on the content in their classes.

Pasnic, S., Bates, L., Brunner, C., Cervantes, F., Hupert, N., Schindel, J., & Townsend, E. (2010). *Ready to learn summative evaluation.* New York, NY: Center for Children and Technology.

Sesame Street appears again, 40 years later, as a federal initiative in literacy incorporates media and technology. Results are modest, but, as with *Sesame Street*, many students are reached.

IV. SOME NEW GOVERNMENT PROPOSALS

Council of Chief State School Officers, Interstate New Teacher Assessment and Support Consortium. (2010). *Model core teaching standards: A resource for state dialogue—Draft for public comment.* Washington, DC: Council of Chief State School Officers.

Federal Communications Commission. *National broadband plan: Connecting America.* Retrieved from http://www.broadband.gov/plan/

Office of Educational Technology, U.S. Department of Education. (2010). *Transforming American education: Learning powered by technology.* Retrieved from http://www.ed.gov/sites/default/files/NETP-2010-final-report.pdf

V. LITERACY AS PART OF THE THEME

Bell, N. E. (2010). *Graduate enrollment and degrees, 1999–2009.* Washington, DC: Council of Graduate Schools. Retrieved from http://www.cgsnet.org/portals/0/pdf/R_ED2009.pdf

A reliable source. About 1.8 million students are currently enrolled in graduate studies. Nearly one-fifth are not U.S. citizens. About three-fifths are females. And last year for the first time, more females than males received doctoral degrees.

Cochran-Smith, M. (1991). Word processing and writing in elementary classrooms: A critical review of related literature. *Review of Educational Research, 61*(1), 107–155. doi:10.3102/00346543061001107

Occasionally a study confirms the remarkable effects of better achievement in the basic curriculum areas. This is one of them. The most important conclusion of this study is that how writing is taught affects the impact of word processing in classrooms. If instruction is poor, the use of technology makes no difference.

Edmonds, M. S., Vaughn, S., Wexler, J., Reutebuch, C., Cable, A., Klinger-Tackett, K., & Wick-Schnakenberg, J. (2009). A synthesis of reading interventions and effects on reading comprehension outcomes for older struggling readers. *Review of Educational Research, 79*(1), 262–300. doi:10.3102/0034654308325998

The review brings together a number of interventions for students in Grades 6 to 12. They varied from a half year to a full year and had an average effect size over 0.80. Essentially provides evidence that doing something is the important thing. On the whole, high schools have usually not developed this sort of intervention. The situation is not hopeless, but action is necessary.

Gaskins, I. W. (2005). *Success with struggling readers: The benchmark school approach.* New York, NY: Guilford Press.

Graham, S., Harris, K. R., & Fink, B. (2000). Is handwriting causally related to learning to write? Treatment of handwriting problems in beginning writers. *Journal of Educational Psychology, 92*(4), 620–633. doi:10.1037/0022-0663.92.4.620

Graham, S., & Weintraub, N. (1996). A review of handwriting research: Progress and prospects from 1980 to 1994. *Education Psychology Review, 8*(1), 7–87. doi:10.1007/BF01761831

Margolis, J., Estrella, R., Goode, J., Holme, J. J., & Nao, K. (2008). *Stuck in the shallow end: Education, race, and computing.* Cambridge, MA: MIT Press.

A passionate book detailing the terrible inequities in access to computers and instruction in the early 2000s. Makes the serious point that access is a part of instruction.

Marulis, L. M., & Neuman, S. B. (2010). The effects of vocabulary intervention on young children's word learning: A meta-analysis. *Review of Educational Research, 80*(3), 300–335. doi:10.3102/0034654310377087

Examined 67 preK and K studies with 216 effect sizes. The average effect on word learning (vocabulary) was 0.88. However, SES was a factor. The higher the SES of the students' parents, the greater the effects.

McGill-Franzen, A., & Allington, R. (2003). Bridging the summer reading gap. *Instructor, 112*(8), 17–19.

Just providing books to low-SES kids made a big difference in achievement and pride.

Royer, J. M., Marchant, H. G., III, Sinatra, G. M., & Lovejoy, D. A. (1990). The prediction of college course performance from reading comprehension performance: Evidence for general and specific prediction factors. *American Educational Research Journal, 27*(1), 158–179. doi:10.3102/00028312027001158

The title says it all. Competence in reading comprehension accounted for 30 percent of student performance in courses in a pair of experiments.

Schwartz, R. M. (2005). Literacy learning of at-risk first-grade students in the Reading Recovery intervention. *Journal of Educational Psychology, 97*(2), 257–267.

A very good treatment of one of the major programs to help struggling first-grade readers. Contains extensive analysis of results.

Suton, R. E. (1991). Equity and computers in the schools: A decade of research. *Review of Educational Research, 61*(4), 475–503. doi:10.3102/00346543061004475

When this was written, access to computers was inversely correlated with SES, and the difference appeared to be exacerbating inequity—this despite the massive Title I program.

Windschitl, M., & Sahl, K. (2002). Tracing teachers' use of technology in a laptop computer school: The interplay of teacher beliefs, social dynamics, and institutional culture. *American Educational Research Journal, 39*(1), 165–205. doi:10.3102/00028312039001165

The ubiquitous presence of technology did not generate a movement toward constructivist teaching. However, teachers who were dissatisfied with normative teaching took advantage of the technology to generate cooperative and project-based teaching.

Zhao, Y., & Frank, K. A. (2003). Factors affecting technology uses in schools: An ecological perspective. *American Educational Research Journal, 40*(4), 807–840. doi:10.3102/00028312040004807

The familiar essentials—leadership, collegiality, and professional development—are outlined and rationalized very well.

VI. ON INDUCTIVE CURRICULUM AND TEACHING

The challenge of the 21st century is to teach students how to learn. Technology greatly expands their possibilities, but teaching students to study inductively, to inquire into content, to take on problems, and to do so cooperatively is the core goal of effective campus and distance courses. There is now ample evidence that the success of ICT depends utterly on the models of teaching and learning that are employed.

Fortunately, we have a massive body of literature on how to do this. What follows is a small sample that includes studies from several perspectives, with some items annotated briefly.

Alexander, P. A., & Judy, J. E. (1988). The interaction of domain-specific and stra-tegic knowledge in academic performance. *Review of Educational Research, 58*(4), 375–404. doi:10.3102/00346543058004375

This is where the teachers' different roles in teaching students to learn conceptually interact. Where teachers have strategic, conceptual control of content, students learn to think conceptually and learn more.

Almy, M. C. (1970). *Logical thinking in the second grade.* New York: Teachers College Press.

One of the greatest studies of the impact of inductive/inquiry/cooperative teaching/learning on the development of the intellect. The discipline-based inquiry approaches to the teaching of science, mathematics, and social studies were brought together for these primary-grade students, and their capacity to think logically—the ability to learn intelligently—increased.

Baumert, J., Kunter, M., Blum, W., Brunner, M., Voss, T., Jordan, A., . . . Tsai, Y. (2010). Teacher's mathematical knowledge, cognitive activation in the classroom, and student progress. *American Educational Research Journal, 47*(1), 133–180. doi:10.3102/0002831209345157

You can't just tell the students to go off and inquire; you have to inquire yourself. A nice study that ties teacher knowledge and use of that knowledge to student learning.

Bloom, B. S. (1984). The 2 sigma problem: The search for methods of group instruction as effective as one-to-one tutoring. *Educational Researcher 13*(6), 4–16. doi:10.3102/0013189X013006004

One-on-one turoring brought out more intensity of inquiry for the students.

Bonsangue, M. V. (1993). Long-term effects of the Calculus Workshop Model. *Cooperative Learning, 13*(3), 19–20.

Conducted with entering students in engineering, this approach improved passing rates dramatically by bringing students together to inquire into the subject matter.

Bredderman, T. (1983). Effects of activity-based elementary science on student outcomes: A quantitative synthesis. *Review of Educational Research, 53*(4), 499–518. doi:10.3102/00346543053004499

From the 1950s through the 1970s, the National Science Foundation and private foundations made substantial initiatives in the sciences, mathematics, and social studies, basing their approaches on the structures of the disciplines and their modes of inquiry. Bredderman brought together 57 studies with 900 classrooms involving three approaches with more than 25,000 elementary school children. The conceptual/inquiry curriculums generated more learning of content, concepts, methods of inquiry, and attitudes toward science. The findings embraced all disciplines as well as intergrated and separate-subject approaches. They applied to children of all grades, all SES levels, English language learners, and students qualified for special education (mild to moderate levels). These findings have been repeated in a variety of studies over the years.

Brenner, M. E., Mayer, R. E., Moseley, B., Brar, T., Durán, R., Reed, B. S., & Webb, D. (1997). Learning by understanding: The role of multiple representations in learning algebra. *American Educational Research Journal, 34*(4), 663–689. doi:10.3102/00028312034004663

A straightforward study. Electronic media expands the ways in which content can be seen and the dimensions by which it can be learned.

Burkham, D. T., Lee, V. E., & Smerdon, B. A. (1997). Gender and science learning early in high school: Subject matter and laboratory experiences. *American Educational Research Journal, 34*(2), 297–331. doi:10.3102/00028312034002297

A large-scale study of tenth-grade achievement in science with a particularly interesting conclusion: that hands-on laboratory experiences, while benefitting all students, were of particular benefit to females.

Calhoun, E.F. (1999). *Teaching beginning reading and writing with the Picture Word Inductive Model.* Alexandria, VA: Association for Supervision and Curriculum Development.

A natural language, inductive approach that is well studied and very effective.

Chamberlin, C. D., Chamberlin, E. S., Drought, N. E., & Scott, W. E. (1942). *Did they succeed in college? The follow-up study of the graduates of the thirty schools.* New York, NY: Harper & Brothers.

The great study that explored whether cooperative, inquiry-oriented schools prepared their students for college as well as delivery-oriented schools did.

Deshler, D. D., & Schumaker, J. B. (1993). Strategy mastery by at-risk students: Not a simple matter. *Elementary School Journal, 94*(2), 153–167.

The most important finding is that students identified as "at risk," including generic problems (e.g., ADHD) and specific problems (e.g., verifiable learning disabilities), can learn strategies that enable them to improve their achievement in the core curriculum areas. The treatments include the Sentence Writing strategy, the TAPE paraphrasing strategy, and the Visual Imagery strategy.

El-Nemr, M. A. (1979). *A meta-analysis of the outcomes of teaching biology as inquiry* (Unpublished doctoral dissertation). University of Colorado, Boulder.

This was one of the most thorough reviews of studies of the implementation of academic reform movement programs in secondary schools. The findings parallel those in the elementary programs, but effect sizes were generally larger.

Eysink, T. H. S., de Jong, T., Berthold, K., Kolloffel, B., Opfermann, M., & Wouters, P. (2009). Learner performance in multimedia learning arrangements: An analysis across instructional approaches. *American Educational Research Journal, 46*(4), 1107–1149. doi:10.3102/0002831209340235

Indicated advantages in self-explanations and the development of experiments. Most important was that all appeared to engage the students positively. Inquiry stood up well.

Fuchs, L. S., Fuchs, D., Hamlett, C. L., & Karns, K. (1998). High-achieving students' interactions and performance on complex mathematical tasks as a function of homogeneous and heterogeneous pairings. *American Educational Research Journal, 35*(2), 227–267. doi:10.3102/00028312035002227

Third- and fourth-grade high-achieving students were assigned to study groups in homogeneous and heterogeneous achievement pairs. The heterogeneously assigned high achievers performed better, confirming the hypothesis that differences are synergistically positive. Heterogeneity generates greater inquiry and conceptual understanding.

Gagné, R. M., & White, R. T. (1978). Memory structures and learning outcomes. *Review of Educational Research, 48*(2), 187–222.

A major piece on cognitive learning. Makes the case that long-term retention and transfer of learning depends on building networks of concepts where information and skills are nested and retrievable.

Johnson, D., & Johnson, R. (1999). *Learning together and alone: Cooperative, competitive, and individualistic learning* (5th ed.). Boston, MA: Allyn & Bacon.

A thorough review of the varieties of cooperative study that generate positive interdependence.

Joyce, B. R., Weil, M., & Calhoun, E. F. (2009). *Models of teaching.* Boston, MA: Pearson.

Discusses a spectrum of models, including combinations that make up the cooperative, inductive, inquiry complex.

Kellman, P., Massey, C., Roth, Z., Burke, T., Zucker, J., Saw, A., . . . Wise, J. (2008). Perceptual learning and the technology of expertise: Studies in fraction learning and algebra. *Pragmatics & Cognition, 16*(2), 356–405.

A group of cognitive psychologists from several universities, including the University of Pennsylvania and the University of California at Los Angeles, are examining how people build categories from a perceptual discrimination point of view. Essentially, discrimination of the characteristics of items is at or near the core of concept development. They are contributing to our understanding, and their work suggests support for the contention that inductive thinking is at the core of higher-order skills.

Klauer, K. J., & Phye, G. D. (2008). Inductive reasoning: A training approach. *Review of Educational Research, 78*(1), 85–123. doi:10.3102/0034654307313402

This study examined the effects of curricula on teaching students inductive processes. Looking at the results of 74 studies involving 3,600 children, it found positive effects on measures of cognitive functioning—essentially, general intelligence—as well as positive effects on academic performance.

Knapp, P. (1995). *Teaching for meaning in high-poverty classrooms.* New York, NY: Teachers College Press.

In 140 high-poverty classrooms, teaching for meaning—comprehension— generated more growth than did teaching with an emphasis on skills.

Kramarski, B., & Maravech, Z. R. (2003). Enhancing mathematical reasoning in the classroom: The effects of cooperative learning and metacognitive training. *American Educational Research Journal, 40*(1), 281–310. doi:10.3102/ 00028312040001281

This study of 384 subjects in eighth grade demonstrated that a combination of cooperative/metacognitive strategies outperformed the effects of either cooperative or metacognitive strategies alone.

Novak, J. D., & Musonda, D. (1991). A twelve-year longitudinal study of science concept learning. *American Educational Research Journal, 28*(1), 117–153. doi:10.3102/00028312028001117

This study followed Grades 1 and 2 students who received supplementary instruction in science concept maps through audio tutorials throughout their school careers. There was considerable variance within the trained group and a control group, but overall, the effects could be seen in science learning throughout the students' time in school.

Rakes, C. R., Valentine, J. C., McGatha, M. B., & Ronau, R. N. (2010). Methods of instructional improvement in algebra: A systematic review and meta-analysis. *Review of Educational Research, 80*(3), 372–400. doi:10.3102/0034654310374880

This study examined five innovations in the teaching of algebra, including technology assists. All improved student learning, but the concept-oriented innovations generated effect sizes double those that focused on procedural content.

Schwab, J. J. (1965). *Biological Sciences Curriculum Study: Biology teachers' handbook.* New York, NY: John Wiley and Sons.

One of the most important designers of science curriculum and accompanying professional development.

Sharan, S. (1980). Cooperative learning in small groups: Recent methods and effects on achievement, attitudes, and ethnic relations. *Review of Educational Research, 50*(2), 241–271. doi:10.3102/00346543050002241

Indicates how complex cooperative inquiry increases conceptual work and reduces the effects of ethnic, SES, and learning history.

Slavin, R. E. (1994). *Cooperative learning: Theory, research, and practice* (2nd ed.). Boston, MA: Allyn & Bacon.

An extensive review, particularly of the structured approaches to cooperative learning.

Slavin, R. E., & Lake, C. (2008). Effective programs in elementary mathematics: A best-evidence synthesis. *Review of Educational Research, 78*(3), 427–515. doi:10.3102/0034654308317473

The best effects were seen in programs that emphasized instructional processes, such as cooperative learning.

Stevens, R. J., & Slavin, R. E. (1995). The cooperative elementary school: Effects on students' achievement, attitudes, and social relations. *American Educational Research Journal, 32*(2), 321–351. doi:10.3102/00028312032002321

Describes a "cooperative immersion" school with positive effects on students, including special education and gifted students who were taught in heterogeneous cooperative groups.

Tennyson, R. D., & Park, O. (1980). The teaching of concepts: A review of instructional design research literature. *Review of Educational Research, 50*(1), 55–70. doi:10.3102/00346543050001055

The concept-attainment model is the focus here. Particularly important is the test of the hypothesis that the learning of concepts facilitates both long-term retention and transfer to problem-solving situations.

Williams, P. B., & Carnine, D. W. (1981). Relationship between range of examples and of instructions and attention in concept attainment. *Journal of Educational Research, 74*(3), 144–148.

VII. FORMATIVE EVALUATION

Ainsworth, L., & Viegut, D. (2006). *Common formative assessments: How to connect standards-based instruction and assessment.* Thousand Oaks, CA: Corwin.

A survey of practices—useful for practitioners who need help as they generate and implement performance testing.

Bloom, B. S., Hastings, J. T., & Madaus, G. F. (1971). *Handbook on formative and summative evaluation of student learning.* New York, NY: McGraw-Hill.

The book that distinguished between formative and summative evaluation, this work has had a major impact on both evaluation and research design.

Calhoun, E. (2004). *Using data to assess your reading program.* Alexandria, VA: ASCD.

This is a comprehensive kit. If you *really* want to know, this will lead you to processes and resources.

Popham, W. J. (2008). *Transformative assessment.* Alexandria, VA: Association for Supervision and Curriculum Development.

A compact treatment of the real difference between normative and performance tests and a full-scale argument for embedded formative evaluation. The apologists for norm-referenced tests have not provided an adequate answer—chiefly because there is no rational defense. But the commercial test makers and their benefactors under No Child Left Behind continue on their obsolete and self-enriching courses.

VIII. DEFINITIONS OF 21ST-CENTURY SKILLS

This body of literature is becoming huge. A good bit of material is on the web, much from the Partnership for 21st Century Skills (www .21stcenturyskills.org), and a number of books have been published on the vision (see, for example, *The Achievement Gap* by Tony Wagner and *Catching Up or Leading the Way* by Yong Zhao). Some of the visionary books will be quite successful. Wagner has a substantial following, and Zhao is building one.

Following are examples from various perspectives:

Darling-Hammond, L., Barron, B., & Pearson, P. D. (2008). *Powerful learning: What we know about teaching for understanding.* San Francisco, CA: Jossey-Bass.

Thin on data, but eloquent in the argument that students need to be taught not just ideas but how to create them. Sponsored by the George Lucas Educational Foundation.

Gardner, H. (2006). *Multiple intelligences: New horizons.* New York, NY: Basic Books.

The eloquent standard for arguments that teaching students how to think is the central goal of education and that it comes in many forms.

Kay, K. (2010). 21st century skills: Why they matter, what they are, and how we get there. In J. A. Bellanca, & R. S. Brandt (Eds.), *21st century skills: Rethinking how students learn* (pp. xiii–xxi). Bloomington, IN: Solution Tree Press.

An early chapter in a book in which two dozen educators discuss the future. This is a succinct statement of the frame of reference of the Partnership for 21st Century Skills.

Wagner, T. (2008). *The global achievement gap: Why even our best schools don't teach the new survival skills our children need—and what we can do about it.* New York, NY: Basic Books.

Despite the outrageous title, Wagner eloquently argues for basic changes necessitated by technological development and the new flat world.

Zhao, Y. (2009). *Catching up or leading the way: American education in the age of globalization.* Alexandria, VA: Association for Supervision and Curriculum Development.

Another eloquent argument for school renewal necessitated by technological developments and global change.

IX. IMPLEMENTATION AND PROFESSIONAL DEVELOPMENT IN ICT

We reference descriptive studies that show that simply providing hardware and software does not result in instructional use in many schools unless there is strong leadership and rich staff development. Too, there is a small but emerging literature on professional development as such in the digital world.

Agee, J., & Altarriba, J. (2009). Changing conceptions and uses of computer technologies in the everyday: Literacy practices of sixth and seventh graders. *Research in the Teaching of English, 43*(4), 363–396.

This type of research is hard to pull off, but the estimates and analysis make good sense.

Allen, I. E., & Seaman, J. (2010). *Learning on demand: Online education in the United States, 2009.* Retrieved from Sloan Consortium website: http://sloanconsortium .org/publications/survey/pdf/learningondemand.pdf

A general view with some data.

Clary, R. M., & Wandersee, J. H. (2009, Fall). Can teachers "learn" in an online environment? *Kappa Delta Pi Record, 46*(1), 34–38. Retrieved from http:// www.kdp.org/publications/pdf/record/fall09/RF09_Clary.pdf

A nice beginning to research on this important subject.

Cuban, L., Kirkpatrick, H., & Peck, C. (2001). High access and low use of technologies in high school classrooms: Explaining an apparent paradox. *American Educational Research Journal, 38*(4), 813–834. doi:10.3102/00028312038004813

The researchers studied use of computers and software for instruction in schools in the heart of Silicon Valley and concluded that access rarely affected curriculum and instruction and that when it was incorporated, it supported rather than changed existing patterns of schooling.

Eisenhart, M., Finkel, E., & Marion, S. F. (1996). Creating the conditions for scientific literacy: A re-examination. *American Educational Research Journal, 33*(2), 261–295. doi:10.3102/00028312033002261

Argues that extensive professional development is necessary and that changes in curriculum guides, standards, and assessments are relatively powerless.

Garet, M. S., Porter, A. C., Desimone, L., Birman, B. F., & Noon, K. S. (2001). What makes professional development effective? Results from a national sample of teachers. *American Educational Research Journal, 38*(4), 915–945. doi:10.3102/ 00028312038004915

Emphasizes the practical, hands-on, site-based delivery of professional development, including self-study by teams.

Hu, W. (2010, February 28). In middle school, charting their course to college and beyond. *New York Times*, p. A19. Retrieved from http://www.nytimes.com/2010/03/01/education/01schools.html

At Linwood Middle School in North Brunswick, New Jersey, 428 sixth graders think about their futures.

Knight, J. (2011). *Unmistakable impact: A partnership approach for dramatically improving instruction.* Thousand Oaks, CA: Corwin.

A careful look at the importance of a collaborative school culture.

Loucks-Horsley, S. (2003). *Designing* professional *development for teachers of science and mathematics.* Thousand Oaks, CA: Corwin.

A very important contributor to professional development discusses design and implementation.

Martin, W., Strother, S., Beglau, M., Bates, L., Reitzes, T., & McMillan Culp, K. (2010). Connecting instructional technology professional development to teacher and student outcomes. *Journal of Research on Technology in Education, 43*(1), 53–74. Retrieved from http://cct.edc.org/admin/publications/feature/JRTE%2043-1%20Martin%2055-76.pdf

One of the early attempts to conduct this difficult type of research. Like most studies on professional development, this one indicates that well-designed professional development, of sufficient length to deal with the content, can make a difference.

Mouza, C. (2009). Does research-based professional development make a difference? A longitudinal investigation of teacher learning in technology integration. *Teachers College Record, 111*(5), 1195–1241.

Another nice beginning to research in the area, this article emphasizes that long-term, well-followed-up modes are effective.

Owston, R. D., Sinclair, M., & Wideman, H. (2008). Blended learning for professional development: An evaluation of a program for middle school mathematics and science teachers. *Teachers College Record, 110*(5), 1033–1064. Retrieved from http://www.yorku.ca/rowston/TCRfinal.pdf

Quellmatz, E. S. (2010). Assessing new technological literacies. In F. Scheuermann & F. Pedró (Eds.), *Assessing the effects of ICT in education: Indicators, criteria and benchmarks for international comparisons* (pp. 121–142). Paris: Organisation for Economic and Co-operative Development.

Schmidt, D., & Lindstrom, D. (2010–2011). Assessing teacher performance in the 21st century. *Journal of Digital Learning in Teacher Education, 27*(2), 41.

A thoughtful reminder that teachers' knowledge of ICT and how to use it will be an important dimension of their competence.

Wei, R. C., Darling-Hammond, L., & Adamson, F. (2010). *Professional development in the United States: Trends and challenges.* Dallas, TX: National Council for Staff

Development. Retrieved from http://www.nsdc.org/news/NSDCstudy
technicalreport2010.pdf

Reports teachers' descriptions of professional development they experienced
and found to be effective. Taken largely from the SASS surveys by the
National Center for Educational Statistics. Emphasizes down-to-earth,
practical experiences of some length that are related to the workplace in an
ongoing fashion. Does not deal with effects.

Resources: Some Places to Go

We can't begin to give you a comprehensive list, but start with these
resources and you will have a good beginning.

Some of the professional organizations are doing a fine job of distribut-
ing ideas and even explicit lesson plans. The National Council for the
Social Studies (see *Social Education* and *Social Studies for the Young Learner*)
and the journals of the National Council for Teachers of Mathematics and
the National Science Teachers Organization are filled with ideas.

Bennett, L. L., & Berson, M. J. (2007). *Digital age: Technology-based K–12 lesson plans
for social studies.* Silver Spring, MD: National Council for the Social Studies.

The social studies thirsts for the world, and ICT is there to help.

ISTE [International Society for Technology in Education]. http://www.iste.org/

Will pour ideas on you if you let them. Has been a great help to the teachers
who have been early users of ICT.

National Science Teachers Association Learning Center. http://learningcenter
.nsta.org/

Teacher's Discovery. Social Studies. http://www.teachersdiscovery-socialstudies
.com/socialstudies.asp.

X. ADDRESSING EFFECTIVENESS OF THE VIRTUAL

Bangert-Drowns, R. L. (1993). The word processor as an instructional tool: A meta-
analysis of word processing in writing instruction. *Review of Educational
Research, 63*(1), 69–93. doi:10.3102/00346543063001069

Thirty-two studies were analyzed. Word processing appeared to help quality
of writing, particularly for the poorer writers, but attitudes toward writing
did not improve as much as did quality.

Bernard, R. M., Abrami, P. C., Lou, Y., Borokhovski, E., Wade, A., Wozney, L., . . . &
Huang, B. (2004). How does distance education compare with classroom
instruction? A meta-analysis of the empirical literature. *Review of Educational
Research, 74*(3), 379–439. doi:10.3102/00346543074003379

The researchers looked at 232 studies with 688 effects. "Overall results indicated effect sizes of essentially zero on all measures" (abstract). However, considerable variance occurred within both distributions. Each approach can generate good or poor results.

Federal Communications Commission. *National broadband plan: Connecting America*. Retrieved from http://www.broadband.gov/plan/

Kulik, C. L. C., & Kulik, J. A. (1991). Effectiveness of computer-based instruction: An updated analysis. *Computers in Human Behavior, 7*, 75–94. Retrieved from http://deepblue.lib.umich.edu/bitstream/2027.42/29534/1/0000622.pdf

An early review with the then surprising finding that average achievement was similar and variance in effectiveness was large for both computer-assisted and face-to-face instruction.

Lewin, T. (2011, March 11). Hearing sees financial success and education failures of for-profit college. *New York Times*, p. A13. Retrieved from http://www.nytimes.com/2011/03/11/education/11college.html

For-profit virtual high schools and colleges are springing up rapidly. The hearings resulted in depictions of unscrupulous fly-by-night "colleges" where federally backed loans support poorly nurtured students with unbelievably high dropout rates. The students don't get an education. Either we pay the bill, or the failing students do over a significant period in their young lives. And the profiteers like Bridgepoint "College" are remarkably well off (its "CEO" took a $20 million salary last year). Perhaps the most astonishing thing is that states accredit these places, as do national "accrediting" agencies. Many preservice teacher education programs that exist only in virtual space have been approved as avenues for certification.

Manzo, K. K. (2010, February 3). Beyond teacher chalk talk. *Education Week Digital Directions, 3*(2), 34–37. Retrieved from http://www.edweek.org/dd/articles/2010/01/08/02whiteboards.h03.html

A cheerleading article, really an editorial, claiming a superiority that is not reflected in scholarly reviews.

Office of Educational Technology, US Department of Education. (2010). *Transforming American education: Learning powered by technology*. Retrieved from http://www.ed.gov/sites/default/files/NETP-2010-final-report.pdf

Sitzmann, T., Kraiger, K., Stewart D., & Wisher R. (2006). The comparative effectiveness of web-based and classroom instruction: A meta-analysis. *Personnel Psychology, 59*(3), 623–664. doi:10.1111/j.1744-6570.2006.00049.x

With a much larger number of studies available for analysis, the findings of this review were remarkably similar to those of the Kulik and Kulik (1991) team.

Tallent-Runnels, M. K., Thomas, J. A., Lan, W. Y., Cooper, S., Ahern, T. C., Shaw, S. M., & Liu, X. (2006). Teaching courses online: A review of the research. *Review of Educational Research, 76*(1), 93–135. doi:10.3102/00346543076001093

Generally, this review's results replicated those of the Bernard et al. (2004) review. The variance in effects of both online and campus courses is striking. The means are important also, with average effects of close to zero. Essentially, where standard content is delivered on campus or online, it can be done poorly or well in either case, *and* the averages are very close to each other.

Wikipedia.org. (2011). The Open University. Retrieved from http://en.wikipedia .org/wiki/The_Open_University

Traces the massive impact of The Open University on access to higher education in the UK—a demonstration of what a carefully organized and planned national distance effort can accomplish. Over 3 million students have been educated in the last 40 years. Courses and course assessments range over most disciplines and include traditional and innovative designs. Evaluation of each student's progress in each course is rigorous and British-traditional.

Zhao, Y., Lei, J., Yan, B., Lai, C., & Tan, H. S. (2005). What makes the difference? A practical analysis of research on the effectiveness of distance education. *Teachers College Record, 107*(8), 1836–1884. Retrieved from http://ott.educ .msu.edu/literature/report.pdf

The researchers report that the aggregate of studies indicates that distance offerings as compared to campus offerings generated about equal effects with respect to the outcomes that were tested. They also confirm that there is considerable variance. In some cases, the effects of the campus courses exceeded those of the distance courses by a considerable margin. In others, the opposite finding appeared. Among other recommendations, the researchers believe that developers need to give attention to the interactive dimensions of distance offerings, particularly instructor contact and interaction among students.

The researchers do not include the massive body of work on The Open University nor on the Childrens' Television Workshop. Importantly, the researchers decided that only 49 journal-reported studies provided data from which an effect size could be computed.

XI. DILEMMAS OF THE SECONDARY SCHOOL

Atkinson, R. C., & Geiser, S. (2009). Reflections on a century of college admissions tests. *Educational Researcher, 38*(9), 665–676. doi:10.3102/0013189X09351981

A super analysis of tests used for college admission. Follows the time when achievement in the core curriculum was common to when aptitude tests were dominant, and the return now to the achievement genre. Presents an analysis indicating that achievement is a better measure of success than the so-called aptitude tests.

Barker, R. G., & Gump, P. V. (1964). *Big school, small school: High school size and student behavior.* Stanford, CA: Stanford University Press.

Coughlin, E. (2010). High school at a crossroads. *Educational Leadership, 67*(7), 48–53. Retrieved from http://learningthenow.com/blog/wp-content/uploads/2010/05/High-Schools-at-a-Crossroads-Ed-Coughlin2.pdf

A clarion call. Discusses the very real possibility that high schools could drift into becoming mere credential-counting institutions as more and more students take distance courses in the core curriculum subjects.

Ewert, S. (2010). Male and female pathways through four-year colleges: Disruption and sex stratification in higher education. *American Educational Research Journal, 47*(4), 744–773. doi:10.3102/0002831210374351

Indicates that academic performance in high school predicts the more disruptive pathways and characterizes the route for a good many males.

Kirn, W. (2010, February 28). Class dismissed. *New York Times Magazine,* 11–12. Retrieved at http://www.nytimes.com/2010/02/28/magazine/28FOB-wwln-t.html

The title underlines the serious drift into a situation where many students use their senior year to take only one or two remaining courses for graduation.

Leithwood, K., & Jantzi, D. (2009). A review of empirical evidence about school size effects: A policy perspective. *Review of Educational Research, 79*(1), 464–490. doi: 10.3102/0034654308326158

The most solid review that confirms the studies that for 40 years have shown that small high schools (see Barker & Gump, 1964, above) generate many effects—academic, social, and personal—better than do most large schools.

Otterman, S., & Gebeloff, R. (2010, August 15). Triumph fades on racial gap in city schools. *New York Times,* p. A1. Retrieved from http://www.nytimes.com/2010/08/16/nyregion/16gap.html

Another episode in the battle to make schools hospitable to everyone.

XII. INTERNATIONAL COMPARISONS

Dillon, S. (2010, March 10). Many nations passing U.S. in education, expert says. *New York Times,* p. A21. Retrieved from http://www.nytimes.com/2010/03/10/education/10educ.html

Testimony before Congress by Andreas Schleicher of the Organisation for Economic Co-operation and Development (OECD). Drawing from the Programme for International Student Assessment (PISA), he asserts that the United States is a year behind other countries. He notes that we have a peculiar mix of decentralization and central control—that schools in other nations are more autonomous.

> We believe he is wrong about this. Per Noon and Noon's article on South Korea, 96 percent of students graduate from high school, the highest percentage in the world. The United States graduates about 70 percent of its students. However, European high schools may operate somewhat like small liberal arts colleges.

Holloway, S. D. (1988). Concepts of ability and effort in Japan and the United States. *Review of Educational Research, 58*(3), 327–345. doi:10.3102/00346543058003327

> Generally supports the Stevenson/Stigler contention that Japanese adults emphasize the role of effort more than do adults in the United States.

Khadaroo, S. T. (2010, June 10). Graduation rate for US high schoolers falls for second straight year. *Christian Science Monitor.* Retrieved from http://www.csmonitor.com/USA/Education/2010/0610/Graduation-rate-for-US-high-schoolers-falls-for-second-straight-year

> The worrisome trend continues—something basic is out of kilter.

PISA studies achievement of reading, mathematics, and science 15-year-old students in the OECD countries and other countries that volunteer to be included.

OECD (Organisation for Economic Co-operation and Development Programme). (2010). PISA *2009 results: What students know and can do—Student performance in reading, mathematics, and science: Vol I.* Paris: Author. http://dx.doi.org/10.1787/9789264091450-en

> Compares achievement in 34 OECD member countries plus other, partner countries. This is the definitive work to date.

Organisation for Economic Co-operation and Development Programme (OECD). (2007). *PISA 2006: Science competencies for tomorrow's world* OECD briefing note for the United States. Retrieved from http://www.oecd.org/dataoecd/16/28/39722597.pdf

Organisation for Economic Co-operation and Development Programme (OECD). (2011). *Strong Performers and successful reformers in education: Lessons from PISA for the United States.* Paris: Author. http://dx.doi.org/10.1787/9789264096660-en

Index

About the Authors

Bruce Joyce grew up in New Jersey, was educated at Brown University, and, after military service, taught in the schools of Delaware. He was a professor at the University of Delaware, the University of Chicago, and Teachers College, Columbia University, where he directed the laboratory school and the elementary teacher education program. His research, writing, and consultation are focused on models of teaching, professional development design and implementation, school renewal, and programs for K–12 beginning readers and Grade 3–12 struggling readers. Primary topics of his speaking and consultation include Teaching Methods, Curriculum and Content, Staff Development, and 21st Century School Renewal. He lives in Saint Simons Island, Georgia, and can be reached via e-mail at brucejoyce40@gmail.com. With Emily Calhoun, his most recent book is *Models of Professional Development* (2010). Thousand Oaks: Corwin.

Emily Calhoun currently focuses on school improvement and professional development, where she combines practice and research. She specializes in the language arts, particularly the teaching of reading and writing in the elementary grades and literacy development K–12, including programs for struggling readers.

She writes and consults on action research, The Picture-Word Inductive Model of Teaching, and ways of incorporating digital technologies into K–12 learning environments through the development of hybrid courses.

She lives in Saint Simons Island, Georgia.

CORWIN
A SAGE Company

The Corwin logo—a raven striding across an open book—represents the union of courage and learning. Corwin is committed to improving education for all learners by publishing books and other professional development resources for those serving the field of PreK–12 education. By providing practical, hands-on materials, Corwin continues to carry out the promise of its motto: **"Helping Educators Do Their Work Better."**

Advancing professional learning for student success

Learning Forward (formerly National Staff Development Council) is an international association of learning educators committed to one purpose in K–12 education: Every educator engages in effective professional learning every day so every student achieves.